THE HEART OF HUNA

LAURA KEALOHA YARDLEY

FOREWORD BY TAD JAMES

Advanced Neuro Dynamics, Inc.

Honolulu, Hawaii

The Heart of HUNA
by Laura Kealoha Yardley, Ph.D.

First Printing 1991

Printed in the United States of America

Published by:

Advanced Neuro Dynamics, Inc.
P.O. Box 3768
Honolulu, Hawaii 96812

Toll Free: (800) 800-MIND
Phone: (808) 521-0057
FAX: (808) 521-0051

Free catalog available on request.

Library of Congress Cataloging-in-Publication Data

Yardley, Laura Kealoha, 1944-
    The heart of Huna / by Laura Kealoha Yardley ; foreward [sic] by Tad James.
        p. cm.
    Includes bibliographical references.
    ISBN 0-9623272-1-2 : $9.95
    1. Shamanism--Hawaii. 2. Long, Max Freedom, 1890-1971.
    3. Bray, David Kaonohiokala, 1889-1969. 4. Kahuna.
    5. New Age movement--Hawaii. I. Title.
    BF1622.U6Y37 1990
    299'.92--dc20   90-27163

Blessings

*This book is lovingly
dedicated to the memory of my grandmother
Adline Poepe Frost, known to me as "Puna,"
and in her lifetime simply as "Mama."*

Judith Sauceda

Aloha Nui Loa

Laura Kealoha Yardley

Nov. 16, 1991
Tucson, AZ

415-381-2844

About the Cross of Light:

This design is a traditional Hawaiian symbol. The four crosses around the outside symbolize the highest energies that represent the four elements: air, fire, water, earth. The cross in the center holds all the others in place and represents the fifth element: spirit.

TABLE OF CONTENTS

ACKNOWLEDGMENTS

It has always seemed as if this book has been guided by a higher force, in particular, the Archangel Michael, who I believe is emerging as the patron Saint of Huna.

All along there have been people who have helped and encouraged me in many diverse ways. I could not list them all, but I wish to acknowledge the following. My parents, Paul and Maili Yardley who gave me the background from which I come; my daughter Cynthia Burgess, whose light and presence accompanies me on the path; Stan Berney, with whom I walked many miles; Bev Powell, who always knows when to call or show up; David Bray Jr., who has helped me with his father's work; Otha Wingo, who carries on the work of Max Freedom Long at Huna Research Inc., and allowed me to quote Long's work; Julius Rodman, who has encouraged and helped me in my studies; Karl Linn, whose early editing helped tremendously; Tad James, Ardie James and Rich Roop, who are responsible for this work finally being published.

FOREWORD

"Let that which is unknown become known," was in a sense a common saying in ancient Hawaii. In the ancient times (kahiko), as in many other cultures throughout the world, the Kahuna were deeply involved in the discovery of the nature of man and the universe. Their search yielded a science of medicine and psychology that was as advanced as that of western Europe and North America at the time. In fact, the teaching of the Kahuna, regarding the nature and the function of the conscious mind and the unconscious mind (la'au kahea), was only recently achieved in western science by Milton Erickson, M.D., (who was a highly respected psychiatrist, psychologist and hypno-therapist) and he reached that understanding only in the 1960's.

When the outsiders (haole) arrived in Hawaii, they mistakenly undervalued all things Hawaiian. Conceited, they took on a parental attitude toward the Hawaiians seeing them only as ignorant savages. It follows that the new arrivals also underrated the practices and procedures of the Kahuna that they saw.

Devoid of the frenzy of "the White Man's burden" and their missionary zeal, we can now forgive them for their embarrassing lapse by granting that the consciousness of the visitors was not far enough advanced to allow them to understand the unthinkable. As the philosopher Ludwig Wittgenstein said, "Whereof one cannot think, thereof one cannot speak." So, if the scholar has not been able to understand the nuances of his chosen field of inquiry what will be the result in how he approaches the subject matter? What will he communicate about the subject?

As you might imagine, therefore, much of what has been written about the science practiced by the ancient Kahuna is incomplete. The fascination of most researchers with Kahuna sorcery (ana'ana), and the lack of understanding of the **full** teaching of the Kahuna, concealed (ho'ohuna) the richness and aliveness of the practices that are the tradition of the Kahuna.

Please understand that there is no blame here, only sadness when we realize that it has taken the world almost 200 years to understand what was being taught then. The tradition of the Kahuna is not as limited as has been portrayed in the literature, for the teaching also included many profound teachings and practices for spiritual illumination (na'auao), and powerful techniques for healing psychological (la'au kahea) and physiological (la'au lapa'au) ills.

There were Kahuna of psychology, medicine, astronomy, agriculture—any field of human activity would have a Kahuna. Yet, due to misunderstanding, the practices of the Kahuna were, in the 1800's, made illegal in Hawaii, and but for a dedicated few, the practices and the teachings might have been lost. We are indebted to those who have kept this knowledge alive. Max Freedom Long (author of a number of books on the subject of Huna) and David Bray, Sr. (a self-proclaimed and publicly practicing Kahuna) are two such keepers of the knowledge, and we are indebted to them both.

These teachings have awaited the time when the people of the earth would be ready to understand them once again—a time when the consciousness of the people would be ready to receive the teachings. Maharishi Mahesh Yogi is reputed to have said, "As the consciousness of the world is raised, the old teachings will once again be revived as the consciousness comes up to the level where the people can understand them again." The profound teachings of the Kahuna order of Kane (to which David Bray, Sr. said he belonged) have not been taught openly in several hundred years. During much of this time, even in Hawaii, they were hidden—known only to a few. Yet, there has been a legend hidden in the teachings of the Kahuna that there would be a time when the original teachings would become known once again. The legend also specified a year and a place, and we believe that this book and those books which will follow in this series are part of the legend.

This book is a first. It is the first time that many of these specific practices have been published. In fact it is the first time that the practices of **any** Kahuna have been published in book form, attributed to their source, and with the blessing of the family. Many practices that you will encounter here have not been taught openly until this publication. Dr. Laura Kealoha Yardley, who is herself part-Hawaiian, hereby sets a milestone with the publication of her extraordinary work. It is for this reason that we are genuinely grateful to include the blessing by David Bray, Jr. ("Daddy" Bray, as David Bray Jr. is called by his family, is a Kahuna as was his father. Daddy is now [1990] well along in years and retired—enjoying life in Hawaii.)

We sincerely hope that this book will clarify and expand the scope of the practices of the ancient Hawaiians. As you read this presentation of some of the practices of the Kahuna, please forgive us for any errors or omissions. If what you read here contradicts what you know, please don't take offense. It is only our thinking (mana'o). May this work clear our vision to tap the power of the infinite

(I'o) so that as we read, we may understand with deep inner insight (ike kuhohonu). In the words of an ancient chant,

Owau keia, o pouliuli.

O powehiwehi.

O ka popolo ku mai a Kane la. Homai ka 'ike i 'ike nui.

'Eli'eli tapu. Noa ia'u. Amama.

In me (oh, Kane) lift up the fire, pierce the darkness

Pierce the darkness of vision.

Pierce the darkness of the unconscious mind, bring the light of Kane to me.

Bring illumination of vision, the great supreme vision to me.

Profound has been the tapu (prohibition). Remove the tapu for me, as I offer this (work) to you (oh, Kane) as a sacrifice.

—Tad James, M.S., Ph.D., author of *Time Line Therapy and The Basis of Personality*, and *The Secret of Creating Your Future*.

BLESSING OF THE BOOK

FROM DAVID BRAY, JR.

Aloha, my name is David Bray, Jr.

Anoai. Anoai. A me aloha pumehana ia oukou a pau.

E pule kakou. (Let us pray.)

E ko makou makua i lo ko o kalani, Ihowa, I'o Kane Ku, Kanaloa, o Lono, na aumakua mai ka po mai no makou ia oukou a pau loa.

We humbly and gratefully acknowledge the blessings granted to us and our fellowship and thank thee for the privilege of being here today. May the blessings of God and the great power be with all those who fully gave of their time, efforts, tolerance, faith and trust to make this possible. In all humility we pray for guidance and divine wisdom, and ask that the spirit of aloha tempered with God's blessings and graciousness be with us all, and that we be granted mana, ike, spiritual blessings, spiritual knowledge, spiritual harmony in all of our work.

Let all of our disappointments, regrets, worries, troubles, doubts, and fears be replaced with the seeds of hope, courage, strength, patience, and love, so that we may be happy in our work.

Left to right: Author Laura Yardley with David Bray, Jr. and Tad James.

CHAPTER 1

THE JOURNEY BEGINS

This is a new age, a period where man's heart will open to balance his intellect, and where he is in contact with his own higher self, the so-called "dead", and the spiritual hierarchy.

This is an age of enlightenment, and you hold in your hands an affirmation of the existence of this new age—for this is a time when, as the Kahuna of old said, all secrets will become known. (Since in the Hawaiian language, there are no plurals, we will be using Kahuna for both singular and plural.)

Simply put, the Kahuna are the priests, priestesses, spiritual teachers of Polynesia; the keepers of the ancient secrets of the universe, the knowledge of which enables them to heal and perform other amazing feats.

The intriguing subject of the Kahuna fascinated me from the very first times I listened to my maternal grandmother, Adline Peope Frost, talk to me of my Hawaiian heritage. During my childhood, the Hawaiian culture was dying out and the older generations were searching to find ways to capture the interest of the young.

My grandmother was highly spiritual and was well known for her ability to interpret dreams. She was loved by all, and people would come to her for advice and interpretation of their dreams. At these times, she would speak to me of the Hawaiian Kahuna, always praising them for their simplicity and dedication. I was seven years old when my grandmother died. In the Hawaiian tradition of knowing when she would die, she called me to her bedside and lovingly told me she would die soon. I stood there, looking at her, and what she said felt so right. She was calm in her acceptance of her death, as she said to me, "Do not mourn my passing my dear. I will be with you always, even after my death. You come from a long line of spiritual women. When the time is right it will all be there. The knowledge will be given you. I will help you and we will be together. I shall be your guide and protector."

My grandmother died, and I did not mourn her death because it was as though she never left me. Her protecting presence surrounded me and yet I did not consciously think about her. It was not until I was thirty-three years old and living in San Diego that her spirit came to me, and made direct contact.

I was in a woman's group at the time and we were doing an art therapy exercise in which we were to begin by writing our name. When I went to write "Laura," I felt a presence enter me and direct my hand to write "Kealoha O Na Ka Puna." (This is my Hawaiian name, given to me by a Hawaiian priest when I was twelve years old and means, "The love of the grandparents is within you.") This presence, which I felt throughout my body, was the spirit of my grandmother, and I soon learned to intuitively feel when she was making contact with me. She asked me to call her "Puna." I began to establish and feel comfortable in a very personal relationship with Puna.

I share my relating with Puna, the spirit of my dead grandmother with whom I share my world as I know it.

This "spirit guide" of mine is intangible, non-material, and cannot be appreciated by the five physical senses unless one is in a condition of heightened awareness. Puna's existence cannot yet be proved to the satisfaction of the pure scientist. Yet, with heightened intuitive senses, Puna is as real to me as the physical world, perhaps even more so at times.

The doubter, who puts belief in spirits down to hallucination or imagination, will not be convinced of their reality until his own experience verifies this to be so. From my own experience I believe such spirit beings exist. It is my desire to share this belief in the hope that it might help others in clarifying their own search for the truth.

The following year, Puna guided me to write this book on the Hawaiian Kahuna. Throughout this work I have been guided by her.

It has taken me two years to complete this book. Most of the time I spent living on the Island of Kaua'i. After a period of intensive research, and as I wrote, I personally spent an intensive period going through a series of spiritual initiations while I integrated what I was learning.

The field of mechanistic science with its materialistic outlook toward life is old and maintains established guidelines. The emerging field of parapsychological science with its holistic vision and spiritual implications is newer and has fewer established guidelines. Those who dare to tread the uncharted country risk the ridicule and misunderstanding of those who have not experienced first-hand the absolute knowing of something for which there is no logical proof. Spiritual research does not present external or objective proof or demand belief. It asks, rather, that one give thought to the ideas being presented. Then, if they fit, they are yours for the keeping.

During the last decade, there has been a great expansion of interest in parapsychological research all over the world. At any time a new and convincing breakthrough may take place which may serve as proof to those who question and doubt such unexplainable phenomena. Today, quantum physicists and mystics are saying the same thing: that all matter is energy and energy is a manifestation of consciousness.

The search for truth is a noble but difficult task. I have searched for the truth about the Hawaiian Kahuna. To solve any problem, *one needs to ask the right question.* It was extremely difficult for me to focus on the question I needed to ask in order to arrive at the truth about the Kahuna. A scientific investigation is a journey in exploring the material world. I began a journey that took me both outward *and* inward. Facts seem to vie with emotions.

Understanding the question makes it easier. It took me a year to understand the question and when I did, it was exceedingly simple: How does the Kahuna heal people? The question was presented to me by Puna and I was left to answer it. This book is that story. It tells the answers that I discovered others had found, and it tells the answers I discovered within myself. It taught me that *any time we have enough information to generate the question, we also have the resources to answer it.* The solving of any problem requires patience, courage, and a particular kind of love directed toward the question.

At first, as I researched the material that was to become this book, I was plagued by worry over Kapu (taboos, restrictions) concerning making public the knowledge of the Kahuna. But as I continued the work, I found that I had the support of the traditional Hawaiian community, as well as David Bray's family. Especially his son, whose blessing appears in the front of this book, and his granddaughter Davida. In retrospect, I guess I didn't really need to worry. After all, isn't this the time for all teachings to become known?

In my case, answering the question became a process of turning inward. This process of turning inward is also a process of turning away from the world for a while, of taking the time that is necessary to get in touch with one's inner nature. This can be different for some people because we humans are used to depending upon feedback from the outer world and the people in it in order to define who and what we are. Learning to live without this feedback and to trust ourselves can be a tenuous process at first. Our models for behaving and defining the world are stripped away and we are left with only a deafening silence which may be awesome to approach.

For those who walk *through* the fear and approach the stillness, they find that the silence they had feared is essentially helping them to know who they are. It is the sound of themselves, no one else; and ultimately, since there is only yourself, this discovery is a very liberating one. Once we are free to discover ourselves, we are free to discover other people without the fear that they will either overpower or submit to us. They will do neither, rather they will simply affirm our own unique individuality.

Liberation, or spiritual freedom, consists of knowing who we are and not being held back in expressing what we know about ourselves. We are all different. To discover who we are, we turn our attention inward and in so doing we discover that spiritual part of ourselves that connects us to Universal Spirit. The Universal Spirit (or I'o, or God, or whatever name you choose to call it) *does* exist. When we find ourselves we find Spirit because Spirit is One and we are all part of It.

Conversely, when we find Spirit, we find ourselves, because Spirit is in us. Peter Cady, the co-founder of the Findhorn Community, said to me on Kaua'i in 1981:

"To follow the spiritual path one must first learn to quiet oneself and listen for the voice within. Then one must have the discipline to follow that inner voice. There is a long period of training and preparation in which one is required to give up everything on all levels: physically, emotionally, and mentally so that

Spirit is put first and one is functioning from a higher level through the personality but not from the level of physical, emotional, and mental desires. One must learn the lessons of faith, strength, ability to take action, laws of manifestation, sensitivity, and understanding."

We go within in order to stand in the presence of Universal Mind/Spirit to find the voice that will answer our questions and lead us to the light. Then we find that Spirit is us.

Over time as I researched the answer to the question, "How do the Kahuna heal?" I discovered that there were two distinct types of people emerging. On the one hand, there were those who scientifically presented the information about what the Kahuna did and theorized about how they did it. On the other hand, there were Kahuna who actually *did* the things that were discussed by the theorists. They were the real practitioners.

As I focused on the central theme of healing, I realized there are those who talk about how healing is done and those who actually heal. To a certain degree, it is difficult for those who talk about how healing is done to actually heal, and it can be difficult for those who heal to talk about how they do it. It became more and more clear to me after I investigated both points of view, that I wanted to find a way to bridge the two, if that were at all possible.

Thus, for me, the problem became one of finding a bridge between the theory and practice of healing. To do this, I decided to select a representative for each point of view. The representative of the scientific theory was easy. There is one man alone who has been responsible for the major scientific exploration of Kahuna healing, and his name is Max Freedom Long. He devoted his life to the study of the Kahuna, and his books form the major basis of our scientific knowledge on the subject.

The representative of the practitioner of healing

Kahuna was given to me in meditation by Puna. She gave me the name of David Kaonohiokala Bray, a self-proclaimed and initiated Kahuna. Bray was also the only person to be recognized by the State of Hawaii as a Kahuna. He was very visible as a Kahuna during his lifetime, and his work continues today.

Long was a scientific investigator, while Bray had the combined gift of intuitive knowledge and spiritual power which enabled him to heal. The difference in the scientific and intuitive types of knowledge is a long-recognized dichotomy. In a sense, it will be likened to the split between the conscious and unconscious knowledge and understanding. I will discuss this in Chapters 5 and 6 after I have presented a detailed investigation of Long and Bray as representational of these two different points of view.

Because it is the ego that separates the conscious and unconscious, Spiritual illumination and the ability to heal cannot be attained without the ego getting out of the way. One has to lose oneself in order to find Spirit. It is the very breakdown of the ego that enables us to *make the transition* from conscious knowledge to unconscious knowledge. This spiritual development is what integrates the conscious and unconscious and results in healing.

Some would say that an individual's ability to draw upon his own inner silence is the measure of his creativity. The Kahuna of Hawaii believe that you do not have to go anywhere else (such as to a retreat in India) or do anything different (such as become a monk) in order to become enlightened. To tap into the vast reaches of soul or universal mind which are always available to each of us, one only needs to turn inside. It is all inside you. The age of gurus is over. It is time for each one of us to stand in his or her light. One needs only to be quiet and listen to the still, small voice within.

The source of the infinite is always there waiting for us; however, we need to take the initiative and tap into it. In order for us to do this, we need to still ourselves. Then we can draw on this source. If one does not draw upon the infinite source, he cannot fully play his part in the drama of the destiny of mankind. Once we learn to listen to the silence, a force is released which illuminates heart, mind, body, and soul. This silence can be perceived as light, the manifestation of which the devout call their inner light. This inner light, or peace, heals and cleanses. The light spreads throughout our very being into our daily lives and manifests itself in a new and changed outlook toward the world. One who listens to the silence and experiences the light is transformed in character, and is able to conceive noble thoughts. Then the hands begin to do acts of mercy, the lips cease to lie, and then the sick can be healed and the ignorant illuminated. Then that person is indeed a Kahuna who has permanent contact with his Higher Self.

My own spiritual initiation and journey within took place on the island of Kaua'i. As I wrote this book, I had to let go of many preconceived ideas. During most of that time, my feelings and thoughts were unclear and I often felt as though I were falling apart. As I was required to give up one attachment after another, I felt totally exposed and vulnerable with no attitudes or beliefs to put between myself and the world. I was stripped bare of my beliefs in order to ultimately lose myself in order to find Spirit within.

I endured pain, and in the process I learned some things about pain. Pain (including the other negative emotions) is not ultimately the path to Spirit. Those who love pain will not find Spirit by seeking pain. Seeking the path of pain only brings more pain. Pain may be a reality and a necessity at times, but the message it brings is one of alert. Pain signals a need to pay attention, to do an instant appraisal of the situation at hand. Pain should never be something to be proud of or pursued for its own pleasure, but rather a warning that something is wrong and out of kilter. Pain is to be understood.

The understanding of the source of pain is an important lesson to learn, since so often we are taught to bear pain and sometimes even to ignore it because it signifies weakness. It does no such thing. Pain is not to be stoically borne. Spirit does not wish to see us in pain. Pain brings a warning. It is to be explored and the cause to be determined. Pain should not be thought of as a noble experiment, but one *can* and should *learn* through pain. Pain is not nice to feel. The alleviation of pain is what is nice to feel.

At times I felt discouraged, depleted, angry, alone, resentful, and confused. Reading the accounts of other people's journeys within helped a lot. I read and can recommend especially *Rolling Thunder* by Doug Boyd (1974), *Lame Deer Seeker of Visions* by John (Fire) Lame Deer and Richard Erdoes (1972), *Black Elk Speaks* by John G. Neihardt (1932), *Undiscovered Country* by Kathryn Hulme (1966), and *Joy's Way* by Dr. Brugh Joy (1979). At my best I sometimes felt like a channel for Spirit, that It had something to say through me. At my worst I sometimes felt as if nothing was worth anything. In my readings I found I was not alone.

Reading *Rolling Thunder,* the story of an Indian medicine man, helped clarify some things for me. I was having difficulty writing about myself within the Kahuna tradition of spiritual healing. It was hard to talk publicly about Puna. Rolling Thunder experienced and talked about these difficulties. For this reason his story was ultimately written by a second person, Doug Boyd. It was nice to know someone else had felt as reluctant to say things about himself as I did.

Once I came to realize I had to be responsible for the mission I had been given and that no one else was going to come along and tell my story, it became easier. I also realized that the times were changing. Old secrets were being shared, and a new generation of spiritual questers and healers was needed to come forth. It was no longer necessary to allow overwhelming humility to hold one back. Certainly the quest I was on was one of discovering the inner light and it made sense to do something with it once I had discovered it. Also, and perhaps more important, I began to realize that I was no different from anyone else and other people must be having similar experiences and would appreciate reading about mine, just as I had appreciated reading about Rolling Thunder's and others.

Rolling Thunder says that it is as if the *profession* of medicine man chooses the medicine man, rather than the other way around. I felt this for myself. It seemed out of my control that my grandmother should choose to pass on her Spiritual knowledge to me and that one day I should be called upon to pass on that knowledge to you through this book.

One last point Rolling Thunder addresses is that of scientifically investigating the subject of healing with spirit guides. He offers the idea that experiments do not cause things to happen. *There is no experiment other than a real situation.* In my case the real situation includes a certain attitude toward what I am discussing and remembering. It includes a certain viewpoint about the relationship between the physical and spiritual world, as well as between the healer and the patient. Absent from the belief are skepticism and judgment. The conditions that exist are simply the conditions that exist when these things happen. They are a part of the experiment, the natural phenomena.

The basic question in my inquiry is: "How do the Kahuna heal?" I start from the basic premise that they do heal and I enter into that reality. Healing starts in the mind, where all reality starts. Everything begins in the mind. Until one has conceived of something in the mind, one is unable to project that thought or a manifestation of that thought out into the world.

Healing is really a process of getting to know oneself and giving up any ego involved. It is the process of being able to become one with the moment and mesh with time, of perfect concentration and belief, even in the face of disbelief and mistrust.

This is an important lesson to be learned during our own growth to perfection: there are certain systems of knowledge which can be passed on to make one's individual search easier and quicker at times. However, these lessons cannot be learned until one has attained a certain level of spiritual development and consciousness. And so they wait until we are ready. Knowing oneself is a matter of getting in touch with one's spirituality.

Kathryn Hulme, in her book *Undiscovered Country* (1966), dealt with her search for her own inner truths under Gurdjieff's guidance. She states that Gurdjieff says that healing results when an individual has found Spirit within.

We are all on a journey, and it is good to be a seeker, but sooner or later you have to find something. When you do it is well to give what you have found—give a gift back to the world for whoever will accept it. When we share we discover a whole new dimension to ourselves.

For a long time I was only a seeker. Writing this book clarified the search for me. The key is to be true to the Self, the true Self within and follow that high, clear guidance that impresses us with the truth. We are perfect, pure, whole and all in one Spirit, one humanity, one life.

CHAPTER 2

THE KAHUNA: "KEEPERS OF THE SECRET"

The word "Kahuna" has been shrouded in the mystic and to many people simply denotes the misuse of power. This is a corruption of the original meaning. In fact in ancient Hawaii, few Kahuna misused their power.

The word Kahu means keeper. Huna means secret. The true meaning of Kahuna is "an expert" in his profession. There were Kahuna of agriculture, building, fishing, astronomy, boat building, sorcery, religion, medicine, psychology and all other specialized fields of knowledge. The term was used as we use the term "Ph.D." today. As you might expect there were more of these Kahuna than the sorcerers.

In order to better understand the Hawaiian Kahuna, we need to first establish an appreciation for the larger social context within which they existed, as well as the historical events which played a part in Hawaiian history and thereby shaped the future of the Kahuna themselves.

Before Captain Cook discovered the Hawaiian Islands

in 1778, Hawaii was a largely self-contained unit isolated from the rest of the world. As in all ancient societies, the religious system played a very important part in the daily life. The Hawaiian religious system was highly developed. Huna, as it came to be called by many, had an advanced understanding of what we would call psychology, and it gave the people a deep spiritual sense of themselves and their place in the universe. They carried these beliefs over into their daily lives and followed a strict code of ethical and ecological practices. Those who did not and who broke tapus (restrictions) were punished accordingly.

The Hawaiians lived very close to the earth and had a great sense of family. The Kahuna, who were the priests, the seers, the healers and medicine men, as well as the experts in the fields of canoe building and other crafts, were an integral part of the daily life of the people. Kahuna were consulted on all sorts of matters. In general, their kind and patient ways, combined with their knowledge and authority, made them well thought of and highly respected. They enjoyed a place of honor in ancient Hawaiian civilization.

Although the majority of the Kahuna were of this type, there were a few who used their power for destructive purposes and for this reason they were greatly feared. However, these destructive and negative Kahuna were in the minority. It is unfortunate that they caused so much attention to be focused upon themselves and established a negative connotation to the word Kahuna in the minds of some people. My focus is on the positive aspects of Kahuna lore.

Thirty five years after Captain Cook discovered the islands, the Christian missionaries started arriving. They took one look at the native Hawaiians and decided that because they could not speak English, had never heard of Jesus, dressed skimpily, and appeared to worship many gods, they were intellectually, morally and psychologically far inferior and needed to be saved. Given their basic assumption that the Hawaiians were ignorant savages, it was hard for the missionaries with their good intentions to look objectively at them and recognize their highly developed psychological and spiritual system. In this way a basic communication problem existed from the start of the Hawaiian acculturation by the Caucasians. In addition to this, the Hawaiians themselves tended to look to the missionaries as their saviors.

One of the first things the missionaries did was to begin to compile an English-Hawaiian dictionary. Up until this time there had been no written Hawaiian language. This was indeed a noble undertaking, but what happened was that much was written down incorrectly or only partially. Leinani Melville, in *Children of the Rainbow* says that the missionaries really had no access to the deeper teachings of Hawaii's wise old priests. In fact, there were none who dared to reveal what they knew to those who were not entitled to know. So the missionaries depended largely for knowledge upon the citizens of the soil (keiki o ka aina) who knew absolutely nothing about the esoteric teachings of the temple priests. The knowledge remained within the priesthood.

In many cases the missionaries did not listen to the common people to whom they did talk. This was because the missionaries held fast to their own beliefs. They could not understand or refused to believe that the Hawaiian religious system could be as highly developed as it was. Eventually the Hawaiians gave up trying to convince the missionaries of what they knew and simply kept quiet; because of this silence, much was not written down. In addition, the missionaries filled in the missing gaps with their own theories and mental creations. All this miscommunication served to create a wide gulf of misunderstanding between the Hawaiians and the missionaries.

After the missionaries arrived, the Hawaiians began dying out rapidly largely because of their inability to establish any immunity to the diseases the white man brought with him. In a sense, they were also unable to establish any kind of immunity to western religious ideas as well. Psychologically, they were overtaken by a confusion that resulted from an inability to assimilate the white man's teachings with their own, and an unwillingness to totally give up either belief system. To a large extent, this situation has persisted into the present, with many Hawaiians not really knowing how many of the old ways they retain and how much of Western Christianity they have accepted for themselves.

Mary Pukui and her co-authors say in *Nani I Ke Kumu* that being part of two worlds, the Hawaiians had to adjust to Western ways. In the process, their everyday ways of understanding their cultural roots were set aside. What was explicit became implicit. Many times, she says, they failed where they could have succeeded, not knowing what course of action to take or whom to trust. Many positive aspects of the Hawaiian culture, concepts such as the importance of the family ("ohana"); the respect for seniors ("kupuna"); cleansing through forgiveness ("kala"); and the regular family therapy sessions ("ho'oponopono") ceased to be everyday practices.

So, the roles of the Kahuna became unclear and in many instances suspect. Eventually the Kahuna all but vanished. However, recently there has been a resurrection of interest in the past and a desire to understand the ways and ideas of the Hawaiians who lived before Captain Cook discovered the islands.

Let us see if we can begin to get a sense of the meaning of the Kahuna, perhaps even begin to understand more by examining the meanings of the word in the Hawaiian language.

The term Kahuna encompasses a wide variety of abilities. *The Pocket Hawaiian Dictionary* defines Kahuna as a priest, minister, sorcerer, expert in any profession. It then goes on to list nine specialties of Kahuna. They are:

1. ***Kahuna ana'ana:*** *sorcerer who practices black magic.*

2. ***Kahuna a'o:*** *teaching preacher, minister.*

3. ***Kahuna ha'i'olelo:*** *preacher, especially an itinerant preacher.*

4. ***Kahuna ho'oulu ai:*** *agricultural expert.*

5. ***Kahuna kalai:*** *carving expert, sculptor.*

6. ***Kahuna kali wa'a:*** *canoe builder.*

7. ***Kahuna kilokilo:*** *priest or expert who observed the skies for omens.*

8. ***Kahuna lapa'au:*** *medical doctor, medical expert, curing expert.*

9. ***Kahuna pule:*** *preacher, pastor, priest, prayer expert.*

(Pukui, Elbert, and Mookini, 1975, p. 49)

The book *Nani I Ke Kumu* (Pukui, Haertig, and Lee, 1975) mentions two additional Kahuna:

1. ***Kahuna pale:*** *the counter-sorcerer, one who says the counter-prayer to ward off a spell.*

2. ***Kahuna po'i Uhane:*** *spirit catching practitioner.*

In his book *The Kahuna Sorcerers of Hawaii, Past and Present*, Julius Scammon Rodman, in his glossary of words used in ancient Hawaiian prayers and temple chants, mentions three other Kahuna:

1. ***Kahuna hoo-pio:*** *sorcery in which the practitioner touched a part of his body, thereby*

causing injury to his victim's body in the same place, a malevolent sorcerer who inflicts illness by gesture.

2. ***Kahuna ki'i:*** *caretaker of images who wrapped, oiled, stored them, and carried them into battle ahead of the chief in command.*

3. ***Kahuna na'au ao:*** *a learned priest who instructed novitiates in wisdom, mystics of science of mind.*

(Rodman, 1979, p. 169)

In addition, Rodman (1979, p. 11) lists fourteen greater divisions of classical black and white orders of sorcery:

1. ***Ana'ana:*** *the art of praying to death.*

2. ***Ho'o-pio-pio:*** *the use of sorcery to bring about death as well as various magical events.*

3. ***Ho'o-una-una:*** *the art of dispatching evil spirit entities on missions of death.*

4. ***Ho'o-komo-komo:*** *the art of creating sickness.*

5. ***Poi-Uhane:*** *mastery of the entrapping spirits.*

6. ***Pule kuni:*** *practicing of a large division of ana'ana in which special objects are burnt as prayers are offered.*

7. ***One-one-ihonua:*** *mastery of a special prayer service.*

8. ***Kilo-kilo:*** *divination.*

9. ***Nana-uli:*** *the art of prophesying the weather.*

10. ***La'au lapa'au:*** *an order of healing priests who employed herbs on occasion, but who healed*

broken bones and other traumas almost instantly
or within a few days, through prayers and
certain esoteric processes.

11. **Kuhi-kuhi puu-one:** *locators and designers of*
    "heiau," or temples.

12. **Makani:** *a wind priesthood with powers over*
    mystic spirits.

13. **Ho'o-noho-noho:** *an order of priests within the*
    "makani" priesthood who were dispensaries of
    spirits of deceased persons, and who could induce
    a "sting of the deity."

That Rodman goes into great detail on categories of harmful sorcerers is indicative of the previous emphasis placed on the negative side of the Kahuna. However, in general, the Kahuna were the ancient specialists of the Hawaiians. They were well trained in various fields:

1. **Doctor:** *Kahuna Haapu*

2. **Diagnostician:** *Kahuna Haha*

3. **Pediatrician:** *Haha Paaoao*

4. **Psychologist:** *La'au Kahea*

Diseases were classified according to those responding to herbs, diet and elimination, spirit power, or physical therapy. Many of the Kahuna practices are logical even today. Each Kahuna had his special preparations and practices, usually handed down from generation to generation.

The most important element in Kahuna healing is the "Aumakua," the god-self or higher self of the individual, and/or other spirit beings above the higher self. All healing, in the Kahuna view, is really nothing more than the result of a natural communion with the Aumakua, of allowing its source energy to flow freely along the original pattern of perfection. All illness or distortion of any kind results from interference with that flow. The most direct healing of body, mind and circumstance comes through consciously involving the Aumakua (higher self, god-self) in one's daily life and thoughts in an open, loving and trusting way.

The practice of aloha (love), which includes the experience and sharing of joy, is the way in which to make this union effective. Joy is life-giving and expansive, and when it is made a part of one's life it automatically releases tension and acts like an invitation to the Aumakua (higher self, god-self) to become a full partner in bringing forth health, happiness and fulfillment. According to Serge King (1979), joyful cooperation with your Aumakua is the best medicine for all ills, the best solution to all problems, and it is the way to achieve personal fulfillment.

The major presenter of the Kahuna tradition to Westerners is Max Freedom Long. In the next chapter we will be looking at his work as an example of a Western version of the Kahuna vision. We will be picking out two important threads of meaning in the tradition—the tradition of healing and the function of the unconscious as an agent of spiritual understanding and healing.

CHAPTER 3

MAX FREEDOM LONG: HIS LIFE AND WORK

Long says of the Hawaiians, that their basic talent was not in mechanics, but in their specific ability to arrive at an understanding of human consciousness, its nature, dimensions and its divisions—the forces through which the elements of consciousness work.

The story of the Huna work begins with Max Freedom Long, born in 1898 and "graduated" in 1971. He devoted the major portion of his life to research on the subject of the Hawaiian Kahuna and pioneered the modern reawakening to the Light of Huna. In 1917 he was a young man in California just out of college, having majored in psychology, and having investigated theosophy and a smorgasbord of various religions.

He took a job teaching on the island of Hawaii in a tiny school on a sugar plantation. He had a native Hawaiian teacher working with him. His job was not demanding and he had much time on his hands. He had already been working on his mental, spiritual, and psychic development, and he had spent much time in meditation and contemplation. As he sat around and talked with the natives, he listened to them tell the stories they had heard from childhood. He heard guarded references to native magicians, the Kahuna, or "Keepers of the Secret." His curiosity became whetted and he began to ask questions concerning the stories he heard. He found, however, that the answers were not forthcoming; and as soon as his interest started showing, the old-timers clammed up.

He was an outsider, a "haole," and they would not confide in him. Could it be, he wondered, that there was some truth to these old stories about how the Kahuna walked barefoot on hot lava, barely hard enough to hold their own weight? How they healed the sick, or solved personal problems or social tangles? He tried to find out, but with no success, for he was met with only a stony silence. He discovered that behind native life there seemed to lie a realm of secret and private activities which were no business of a curious outsider. He also learned that the Kahuna had been outlawed since the early days of the Christian missionaries and that any suspect activity would definitely be done undercover and not about to be exposed to any white man.

Max was inclined to look upon stories of the use of magic, instantaneous healing, and the walking about of spirits and lesser gods with great suspicion. However, he was fascinated by the stories, and if he could not get the natives to discuss them he could at least read about them in books on the subject. He set about reading everything he could find. After three years of reading and trying to glean information from the natives, Max decided to go back to the mainland. He gave up the idea of finding out the secrets of the Kahuna as hopeless. He went first to Honolulu, where he had heard of the famous Bishop Museum, and decided to pay it a visit. He tells the story in *The Secret Science Behind Miracles* (Long, 1954b).

He says that the purpose of his visit was to try to find

someone who could give him an authoritative answer to the question of the Kahuna which had plagued him for so long. His curiosity had grown too large to be comfortable, and so he was a man on a mission. He finally heard that the curator of the museum had spent most of his years delving into things Hawaiian. So, Long hoped that he would be able to give him the truth, coldly, scientifically, and in an acceptable form.

The curator, William Tufts Brigham, replied in effect: "I've been waiting for you for forty years." Instead of giving him the negative answer he had been expecting, Dr. Brigham asked him penetrating questions and encouraged Max to tell him all he had learned and theorized. At age eighty-two, Dr. Brigham had spent forty years trying to learn the secrets of the Kahuna, and using the same scientific methods he had used in the scholarly research for which he was famous. For four years Max studied with Dr. Brigham, who taught him in careful detail the basic principles that he had worked out. These principles were the basis Max eventually used in recovering the ancient "magic."

"Always keep watch for three things in the study of this magic."

Dr. Brigham repeated over and over so that they would sink into Max's consciousness and never be forgotten.

"There must be some form of consciousness back of, and directing, the process of magic. There must also be some form of force used in exerting this control, if we can but recognize it. And last, there must be some form of substance, visible or invisible, through which the force can act. Watch always for these, and if you can find any one, it may lead to the others." (Long, 1954b, p. 14)

Dr. Brigham died in 1926 and Max stayed in Hawaii for five more years, doing painstaking research and trying to support himself financially. In 1931 he admitted defeat, or so it seemed, and returned to California, where he ran a camera shop. There he got away from the minute details of the problem that had captured his interest for fourteen years, and became involved in the process of running a business. It was more like a shift in consciousness. In the back of his mind, things were gelling. All the while he kept an occasional eye out for any new development in psychology that would give him a new clue. When the time was right, he knew the light would go on and everything would fall into place. He describes his illumination in this way,

Then, in 1935, quite unexpectedly, I awakened in the middle of the night with an idea that led directly to the clue which was eventually to give the answer. The idea that had struck me in the middle of the night was that the Kahuna must have had names for the elements in their magic. Without such names they could not have handed down their lore from one generation to the next (Long, 1954b, p. 16).

The result was a study of the *root-words* of the Hawaiian language for the clues to what the Kahuna conveyed in ancient chants and prayers that had to be recited exactly the same every time. Remembering Dr. Brigham's three elements as a basis for discovering the secret behind the miracles, Max was able to identify the first two before the year was out, but it took six more years to identify the last one. The consciousness was the Aumakua (higher self, god-self), the force used was Mana (life force, power, chi, ki, prana), and the invisible substance through which the force acted was Aka (etheric substance).

In the late 1930's the first report of Max Freedom Long's findings on the ancient Kahuna lore was published in England. This book, *Recovering the Ancient Magic*, had an unusual history. The printed pages were ready for binding and the first copies were being shipped out from the publisher when the building was destroyed by a bomb. This was during the German blitz in London. All remaining copies and the printing plates were destroyed. Information about the Huna lore was not to be distributed by this early volume. However, by 1945 sufficient interest was shown in Max's work that he found it necessary to answer his correspondence by way of a mimeographed letter. At that time he established the Huna Fellowship as a non-profit, educational and religious organization. It was chartered in California. Three years later, he established the Huna Research Associates as a membership organization for research and information on Huna, for which mimeographed bulletins were sent out to members every two weeks.

In 1948 *The Secret Science Behind Miracles* was published, and this, along with regular bulletins, formed the basis of the Huna research work at this time. During this period membership ranged between 300 to 400 and all expenses were met by the members. In addition, Max corresponded all over the world with well-known researchers and many fine workers.

In 1953 Max published *The Secret Science at Work*, which was more of a practical textbook. It gave the background information in *The Secret Science Behind Miracles*, as well as the experimentation and methods of procedures with which Max had been working. Then, in 1954, he published *Growing into Light*, in response to a request from a reader that he write a "simple" little book of the things that had inspired him from day to day during his long years of research. In the introduction of *Growing Into Light* he writes,

Yes, I will gladly share with you the thoughts and ideas that have helped me to grow into Huna. I will

give you the exercises and the affirmations which I have used, and I shall also try to be very simple in all that I have to say—but this will be very hard. Only the very great have been able to attain simplicity, and I am not in this category... It is not easy to discuss in simple terms the very great ideas which the enlightened sages of ancient times have given us as a heritage... Undoubtedly there are many veiled meanings which I have not yet come to know. The work continues steadily in this search to which I have dedicated myself (Long, 1954a, p. ix.)

In 1958 Max announced that he was phasing out the Huna Research Association Bulletins in order to devote more time to the writing of books. At this time *Self-Suggestion and the New Huna Theory of Mesmerism and Hypnosis* (usually designated simply as *Self-Suggestion*) and *Psychometric Analysis* appeared. However, by this time interest had increased and Max found it necessary to keep up with his correspondence on all the news and research by publishing a new series of bulletins which he called *Huna Vistas.*

This publication continued monthly for 98 issues until just shortly before Max's death, which he referred to rather, as his "graduation." During these last years Max continued his research and wrote *The Huna Code in Religions* (1965), which is a major contribution to the subject of comparative religion and psychology. He included a few pages of the Hawaiian language dictionary by Andrews published in 1865.

Max "graduated" on September 23, 1971, a month before his eighty-first birthday. The task of continuing the Huna work was passed to E. Otha Wingo, who assumed the position of director of the Huna Research Associates. He reprinted several early treatises of Max's and in 1973 completed the first correspondence course on the Fundamentals of Huna Psychology, entitled *Letters on Huna.*

The Huna Research Association continues today under the auspices of Otha Wingo and membership is open to all interested people. Since 1975, the Association has sponsored annual Huna Seminars all over the United States and Canada. Plans are in the works to publish other manuscripts Max left behind. So the work that Max Freedom Long carried forth from his chance meeting with Dr. William Tufts Brigham at the Bishop Museum in 1920 continues today, seventy-one years later, years after Long himself "graduated."

Max Long lived by and believed in the ancient command of the Kahuna: "Let that which is unknown be known." Down through the ages, in addition to the outer teachings of most of the great religions, there have also been secret or inner teachings which were revealed only to adepts or initiates, for whatever the reasons may have been. Jesus himself taught in parables and told his listeners that their meanings would only be clear to those who could understand. Max Long believed that the world was ready to receive the shining light of Huna and that the time had come. He very much believed there were to be no more secrets and that the light of Huna could be known by all.

What is Huna? It is the esoteric system of knowledge Long found revealed in the Hawaiian language itself when he deciphered the code and revealed its mysteries. It is a *religion* in the sense that it inspires man to attain spiritual perfection and find Spirit within. It is a *science* because it deals with the physical world and its techniques produce repeatable results. It is a philosophy of life because it embodies a strong code of ethics. Some consider it magic because it works with unseen forces which are nevertheless real, and it produces results not fully understood by some.

Long described Huna as a "psycho-religious" structure. He felt it was *not* a religion in the true sense. He pointed to Professor Paul Tillich of Columbia University, a

Professor of Philosophical Theology, who defined religion thus: "Religion is the relation to something ultimate, unconditioned, transcendent. The religious attitude is a consciousness of dependence, surrender, acceptance" (Long, 1954b, p. 310). Huna, he stated, had none of that. There is no reverence for gods and the High Self is not a god, as we shall see. He called it a "psycho-religion" because it included so much that has always been considered a part of religion.

Long considered Huna a science in the strictest sense of the word. The word science means "knowledge," and implies a systematized body of knowledge, presumably useful. The science of psychology and the science of psychism are not a part of religion. They are science. Huna falls into the area of psychological sciences—the study of the complete make-up and function of an individual (his psyche). To quote Long,

What I mean, therefore, by Huna Psychology is a practical system of knowledge of What You Are, what You as a whole person consist of and How you can fulfill your ultimate potential by understanding and using that knowledge for more abundant and effective living. What makes it HUNA Psychology is that we are using as our frame of reference the Ancient Wisdom derived from the actual practices of the rigorously trained specialists of old Hawaii, the Ka-Huna, knowledge which the "modern" psychologist has only come to recognize in recent years—or even yet does not recognize. As a case in point, no one apparently even heard of the unconscious mind (at least in academic circles) or even suspected its existence until Sigmund Freud wrote of his "discovery." Yet, the Kahuna of ancient Hawaii knew not only of its existence, but its special and important functions and how to harmonize it with the other functions of his psychological make-up. The word "Huna" means secret. So, you are studying here the SECRETS of ancient psychological wisdom (Wingo, 1973, p. 2).

Although Huna is not a religion, it is not in conflict with any religion. It does not ask that you believe in any dogma, but rather that you put the principles to work for yourself and see if they work. Then, if you use them and they work, make them a part of your normal way of life. Knowledge of Huna will help you understand yourself, and as a consequence of knowing yourself, the great light of understanding will be thrown upon every part of your life.

As a philosophy of life, the basic tenets of Huna as taught by Max Freedom Long are "No Hurt—No Sin" and "Serve To Deserve." Sin is defined as harming another person. This is a simplistic way of describing unconditional love as a way of life.

As for the association that Huna might have had with magic, Long had definite ideas on the subject. First, he felt the word "magic" had negative connotations associated with it to the extent it has become almost synonymous with the term "black magic." Long's Huna was the very antithesis of such practices.

Technically "magic" is the use of the powers you possess to gain something which you desire (hence the idea arose that the "magician" acquired certain "supernatural" powers which he made use of to obtain BY FORCE certain favors from a divine, or "supernatural" being—and since this is supposed to be impossible with man's ordinary ability, the practice was considered to be "magical" or "miraculous)." How different Huna is—you will learn to use "powers" that are quite natural to you (but perhaps latent and unused up to now) for the purpose of fulfilling desires or obtaining certain "favors"—but it will not involve the use of "supernatural" force against a supernaturally divine being. Only by failing to understand how this is accomplished can any "magical" qualities be attributed to Huna (Wingo, 1973, p. 3).

Most significantly, it has been found that the principles of Huna not only provide a logical and consistent explanation of what some have heretofore called magic, but when they are *applied* they produce results. The primary result that the ordinary Kahuna practitioners worked for was healing. Depending upon their specialty, they would work toward healing of different types: healing of the body, healing of the mind, healing of the spirit, or healing of social or financial difficulties.

To better understand Long's concept of Huna, let's take a look at a course in the principles of Huna, written by Otha Wingo in *Letters on Huna* (1973). The course embodies all the concepts that Long covered in his writings. References will be made and you will gain the tools necessary to produce your own results. It is not a prerequisite to believe in Huna, you only need to be willing to try it.

LESSON 1: HA PRAYER

Take a deep breath, quickly through the nose, as deep a breath as you can without becoming uncomfortable, and then exhale slowly through the mouth making the "HA" sound. Sit back and feel yourself relax. Take a few more deep breaths and as you exhale, let the release of the breath symbolize to you the releasing of your tensions and troubled thoughts. You will notice that in addition to the release of tension there is a sharpened awareness with which you will focus your attention on this discussion of the basic Huna principles.

Huna was originally a specialized system of knowledge and was kept secret by those who possessed it. Ancient Hawaiian Kahuna passed on the knowledge only to specially chosen students, usually a son or a daughter. Truth will be intuitively recognized, however, if you are ready for it. Huna works. Huna offers an understanding of how you can achieve an effective and harmonious way of living.

Take a moment and relax. Go within and meditate. The following meditation is used world-wide and expresses the Huna idea of Light.

THE GREAT INVOCATION

From the point of Light within the Mind of God
  Let light stream forth into the minds of men.
    Let LIGHT descend on earth.

From the point of Love within the Heart of God
  Let love stream forth into the hearts of men.
    May Christ return to Earth.

From the center where the Will of God is known
  Let purpose guide the little wills of men—
    The purpose which the Masters know and
    serve.

From the center which we call the race of men
  Let the Plan of LOVE and LIGHT work out
    And may it seal the door where evil dwells.

Let LIGHT and LOVE and POWER restore the Plan
  on Earth.

(Wingo, 1973, p. 7)

Knowledge is power. If you are not using Huna, you are working too hard.

LESSON 2: THE TEN ELEMENTS OF HUNA

Psychic ability is not necessary for the use of Huna. Such ability is natural to everyone and is developed to a greater extent in those who work on it. Since Huna involves the study and practice of universal laws, most people discover that the intuition (meaning "teacher within") becomes strong and "psychic" or spiritual awareness develops. This ability is the by-product of such study and not to be considered extra-sensory (outside the senses) or super-natural.

What follows here is the Huna account of the structure of the conscious and unconscious mind and their relation to the spiritual or High Self. This is a combination of both psychological and spiritual explanations of the basis of human behavior and is also a description of *both* healing *and* harmful energies within the individual. The good Kahuna worked with healing energy and the bad Kahuna would try to disrupt the system in order to produce harm and imbalance, which led to disease.

You are more than a body. Wingo quotes Long,

Because you are conscious of your own existence, you realize that you are alive and that a process of thinking is taking place. You are aware of your body and its various functions, both voluntary and involuntary. The part of you that is aware of these things— the real you, so to speak— enables you to be conscious of the fact that you exist as a spiritual or psychic "person" in addition to the body in which you seem to live. It is natural, therefore, to speak of YOU and your body, as two parts, whether they are actually thought to be separate or not (Wingo, 1973, No. 2, p. 3).

Psychology since Freud recognizes both an unconscious and a conscious mind. For the purpose of discussing the psyche (the focus of the study known as psychology), we may speak of two minds or two selves—the conscious mind self and the unconscious mind self. The Kahuna had names for these two selves. They called the conscious mind "Uhane" (or the middle self) and the unconscious mind self the "Unihipili" (or the low self). The "Uhane" is the conscious part of man with the power to reason. The "Unihipili" is the animal nature where the emotions reside.

In addition to these two parts of man, there is a third that the Kahuna called Aumakua (higher self, god-self). Sometimes called "superconscious," to the Kahuna it was the older, utterly trustworthy parental spirit. In a religious sense it may be likened to God or a sort of Guardian Angel. It is the part of man that helps upon request but never interferes with the free will. It is this High Self that brings all desired conditions into reality.

All three selves play their distinct and quite unique role in the life of each of us. The important thing is that they are working in harmony and cooperate with one another. As long as this is the case, our life runs smoothly and miracles appear to happen.

Each of these three selves of man has a duplicate which the Kahuna referred to as "kino-aka" (invisible but real shadowy bodies).

This invisible "aka" substance formed a sort of pattern or aura around each of the three selves, keeping the blueprint intact, but capable of changing shapes temporarily or permanently to form a connecting thread between the inner or low self, the middle self, and the High Self. Since "aka" has a sticky quality and stretches without breaking, when contact is made between two persons, a long sticky thread is drawn out between the two, like a thin spiderweb, and the connection remains. Further contacts add other "aka"-threads and these are braided together into an "aka" cord, resulting in strong rapport between the two individuals.

Such a bond must be kept strong—the "aka" cord

strongly braided—between the low self and the middle self, and between the low self and the High Self, in order for the three to work harmoniously together (Wingo, 1973, No. 2, p. 5).

Once the three selves are working together, we have perfect communication among the three selves, and this is at the very heart of the secret of Huna. Our goal, as a conscious middle self, is to learn about, establish contact with, and work harmoniously with our low self and our High Self. The union of the three selves creates harmony and balance.

Modern psychology has recently recognized the conscious and unconscious mind, but has failed to recognize the High Self. Huna clarifies the distinction among the three selves and explains their unique qualities.

The Kahuna recognized the nature of vital force, which they called Mana (life force, power, chi, ki, prana). It was the essence of life itself and the basis of all thought processes and bodily activities. Their symbol for Mana was water. Water, like Mana, may flow, fill things, or leak away.

The Kahuna associated all thinking process with Mana. The word "mana-o" means "thinking, " the "o" added to show that the process is one of using Mana to produce thought. As each thought is formed, it is given its shadowy body ("aka") and is fastened by a thread of the same substance (or by direct contact, perhaps) to thoughts which come before it (Wingo, 1973, No. 2, p. 7).

The low self takes Mana from food and air and stores it in its "aka" body and then shares it with the middle self and High Self. Each self has a particular kind of Mana that it uses. The Mana of the low self is the vital force, sometimes called prana, or universal life force. It is a low-voltage energy produced by the body. It can flow over aka threads through the body or to that of another person. The Mana of the middle self is called Mana-mana because it is changed in some subtle way when used by the middle self and doubles in strength. It is a higher voltage and frequency. Mana-mana is used by the middle self in all thinking and willing activities. It is used by the middle self to command the low self. The Mana of the High Self is called "Mana-loa" and is the highest form and voltage of Mana. Mana-loa is a transformed, supercharged (in both voltage and frequency) Mana used by the Aumakua (higher self, god-self) to change the invisible pattern into reality. Understanding the three types of Mana enables a person to better use and control them.

To summarize, there are ten elements in the Huna psychology. There are the three selves, their three Aka (etheric substance) bodies, the three levels of Mana (life force, power, chi, ki, prana), and the physical body. The physical body is the vehicle and instrument of the three selves.

We begin with the three selves—the Unihipili (lower self, unconscious mind, body-mind), the Uhane (middle self, conscious mind), and Aumakua (higher self, god-self). (See Chart 1) First, the Unihipili is the inner self, the unconscious self. It is where the memory and emotions reside. It is illogical, forming exact, literal, deductive conclusions. The Unihipili controls body functions and "aka" threads and thought-forms. It responds to suggestion. It is the seat of conscience, relies on the five senses and can use telepathy.

Second, the middle self, or the Uhane is the conscious, rational mind self. It possesses full reasoning powers but not memory. It has willpower and imagination, and programs the conscience. Only the middle self can sin, and the only sin is to willfully hurt another person. The Uhane is the ordinary, everyday, rationalizing part of man.

Third, the Aumakua (higher self, god-self) is the "utterly trustworthy parental spirit", or the superconscious.

CHART 1: THE TEN ELEMENTS OF HUNA PSYCHOLOGY

The 3 Selves	3 Levels of Mana	3 Aka Bodies
HIGH SELF or AUMAKUA	**MANA-LOA**	**KINO-AKA**
"Utterly trustworthy Parental Spirit", "Superconscious"	Highest form of Mana. Highest "voltage."	Shadowy body of the High Self.
"Realization", including past, present, and the crystallized part of the future. "Guardian Angel" concept. Symbolized by the Sun. In contact with higher powers.	A transformational, super-charged Mana used to change the invisible pattern into reality.	Shown as "halo" in art.
MIDDLE SELF or UHANE	**MANA-MANA**	**KINO-AKA**
"Conscious self", Rational Mind, "Persona"	Double strength Mana. Higher "voltage".	The invisible pattern of the Middle Self.
Full reasoning powers. Will power. Imagination. No memory. Programs "conscious". Only Middle Self can "sin". Rationalization. Ordinary, everyday thinking.	Used by Middle Self in all thinking and "willing" activities.	Less dense.
LOW SELF or UNIHIPILI	**MANA**	**KINO-AKA**
Inner Self, Real Self, Deep Self, "Unconscious" Self	Vital force, "Prana", universal life force, low "voltage" energy produced by the body.	Physical/etheric body. The energy body of the Low self.
Memory and emotion. Illogical. Controls body functions. Controls aka threads and thought-forms. Subject to suggestion. "Conscience". Generates all emotions. Relies on five senses. Telepathy.	Can flow over aka threads, flow through to body, or to that of another person.	Aka sticks to whatever it touches. Draws out thin, aka thread. Conducts Mana.

The Physical Body
The Vehicle and Instrument of the Three Selves.

It "realizes" things by intuitive knowing, including past, present, and the crystallized part of the future. It is the "Guardian Angel" and is in contact with higher powers as well as other High Selves, known as the "Poe Aumakua," the "Great Company of High Selves." These are the three selves.

The three bodies of Aka (etheric substance) correspond to the three selves. At each level, the etheric bodies are called "kino-aka". First, the Aka body of the low self is "kino-aka." It is the etheric body and its aka sticks to whatever it touches and draws out thin, Aka threads. It also conducts Mana (life force, power, chi, ki, prana). Second, the Aka body of the middle self is the invisible pattern of the middle self, and is less dense than that of the low self "kino-aka." Third, the Aka body of the High Self is the shadowy body of the High Self, often depicted as a halo in art. These are the three "aka" bodies of the three selves of man.

Next, these three selves, each possessing an Aka body, also possess a certain Mana. First, the Mana of the low self is called plain mana. It is the vital force, or "prana," or universal life force. It is a low-voltage energy produced by the body. It can flow over Aka threads, through the body, or to the body of another person.

Second, the Mana of the middle self is called Mana-mana. It is double strength Mana of a higher voltage and frequency and is used by the middle self in all thinking and willing activities. Third, the Mana of the High Self is called Mana-loa. It is the highest form and voltage of Mana. This transformed (higher voltage, higher frequency), supercharged Mana is used to change the invisible pattern into reality.

These are the three levels of "mana," used respectively by the three selves. So thus we have the physical body, the three selves, the three bodies, and the three types of Mana: the ten elements of Huna.

LESSON 3: INCREASING MANA

If we are in good health and not starved, there are certain exercises we can do to accumulate an extra large and powerful charge of Mana. We can then use this charged Mana to heal others or ourselves, or to send a prayer with particular power from the Unihipili (lower self, unconscious mind, body-mind) to the Aumakua (higher self, god-self).

The Uhane (middle self, conscious mind) through action of the mind and exercising its will, can command the low self to take in more air and cause more blood sugar to be burned, thereby creating more Mana. The low self learns to do this and we can help it by using the voluntary muscles and starting breathing more deeply.

The Kahuna used water as a code word or symbol for Mana. To accumulate a surcharge of Mana they would breathe deeply and visualize Mana rising like a fountain. They imagined their body as the fountain and the water rising higher and higher until it overflowed all over the body. This can be done through physical exercise or mentally holding the picture.

Producing more vital force creates a sense of well-being, sharpening the mind and making the senses more acute. In addition, when one has learned how to accumulate a surcharge of Mana, one can then learn how to direct it to perform what seem like miracles.

To obtain its needed Mana, the High Self contacts us of its own accord in our sleep, by way of the connecting cord of Aka (etheric substance) material. The vital force that is taken is stepped up to the higher voltage Mana of the High Self and returned as a compensating force which is vital to our well-being and health. This is pictured as a shower of Mana falling from the rising fountain as a "rain of blessings." Daily and hourly contact may be maintained with the High Self by consciously sending it Mana and waiting for the blessings to fall.

LESSON 4:

ACCUMULATION AND USE OF MANA SURCHARGE

The Kahuna were very practical in their outlook. To them, life was consciousness plus Mana plus the invisible Aka (etheric substance). Mana alone was not life. It was the force used by the particular self, lower, middle, or higher. Remember that there are three types of Mana corresponding to the three selves. Remember also that the low self needed to provide Mana to the Aumakua (higher self, god-self), which it would then transmute into its own particular Mana in order to use it to effect changes requested by the low self through prayer or other techniques.

The first step was deciding what was wanted. Then thought-forms of the desired result were made to be sent to the High Self to be used as molds into which the future would be cast by the High Self. For success at this task, the High Self must be supplied with mana by the low self. At the direction of the middle self, the low self accumulates a *surcharge* of mana for this purpose.

In the accumulation of a surcharge of Mana, this part of making the prayer action consists of three steps:

1. *Deciding what you will do with the surcharge in the way of healing, changing the future, or prayer request.*

2. *Giving the order to the low self to do the actual work of accumulating the surcharge.*

3. *Making some physical stimulus to get the low self to go to work, such as exercises or breathing postures. Breathing itself is a form of exercising. In accumulating a surcharge by breathing without physical exercise, the supply is held instead of being used up in muscular activity. It*

is therefore available to be used in the prayer
action or in the laying on of hands to heal.

The low self needs to be impressed with what we want and then we need to let go and trust the low self to do its job. Prayer is not just thinking. It is a combination of thinking *and a gesture* of actual physical movement of the Unihipili (lower self, unconscious mind) in the body by which Mana is created and given to the High Self. It is good to develop a physical ritual which is definite and repeatable so as to get the attention of and impress the low self.

Mana is living force. It can and will obey the commands given to it. These commands are first given by the middle self to the low self, who then accumulates the Mana and directs it to the High Self. Here it is transformed into Mana-loa (high mana). The low self also sends its mana to the middle self, to be used as "Mana-mana", or will. (This is energy used by the conscious mind).

LESSON 5: EFFECTIVE PRAYER

Let us discuss the five steps to an effective prayer or prayer-action to a Higher Intelligence, in this case the High Self. To begin with, let's look at the word "prayer." The intrinsic meaning of prayer is "an earnest request." Long uses the term "prayer-action." To quote him:

The expression prayer-action is closer to our meaning here. In the Hawaiian language, there are two significant words for prayer:

(1) "waipa," meaning literally "to divide water." Water is the Huna symbol for "mana" or vital force and thus prayer refers to the use of mana in the various functions of the three selves.

(2) "pule," meaning "to send forth" thought forms to

the High Self via the flow of mana along the aka cord. So when I speak of prayer or prayer-action, I am referring to a carefully worked out blueprint for what we wish to be built into our lives, together with the appropriate implementation of that design (Wingo, 1973, No. 5, p. 1).

The five steps to an effective prayer or prayer action are:

1. **PREPARATION:** *Preparation for the act of prayer, which involves careful consideration of the new and desired conditions which one wishes to have brought into action. One may ask for health, happiness, prosperity, including specific manifestations of each of these categories; however, one must remember to include service to others and should never do anything or ask anything to hurt another unjustly. One must decide upon the future, plan it in as much detail as possible, and then set about to bring the desired condition into reality.*

2. **BUILD THOUGHT FORMS:** *Building a complete set of thought-forms of the new future, through visualization and with the use of a physical stimulus to impress the low self.*

3. **ACCUMULATE & SEND MANA:** *Accumulation of a sufficient supply of Mana (as discussed in the previous lesson) and the sending of it along the "aka" cord to the High Self.*

4. **DAILY PRACTICE:** *The follow-up, or daily review of our desires. We keep them thriving by daily sending "mana" to the High Self. The Kahuna symbolized this as to grow the seeds (thought forms) by sprinkling them with water (mana) until they bear fruit as actual conditions*

as the future becomes the present.

5. ***CLEARING THE PATH:*** *Removing any blocks held by the low self to prevent the asked-for conditions to be made manifest. These blocks are caused by such things as guilt, fear, fixations (fixed ideas held by the low self).*

LESSON 6: WHAT TO PRAY FOR

The Kahuna were simple men and their system reflects their simplicity and practicality. Their ideal was the normal condition: normal health, normal supply of the necessities of life, normal relations among the three selves in each individual. For the Kahuna, the normal condition was the happy one. To be happy, one enjoyed the normal inter-workings among the three selves, showed love and kindness toward others, and observed the rule of no hurt. Remember, the only sin was to hurt another individual. Within this framework, anything could be asked for that was normal and good for one and for those around one.

The Kahuna taught that our goal on earth is to attain unity of the three selves, with none taking dominance, but each doing its part. Therefore, each had a specific lesson to learn. The low self must learn not to hurt others (No hurt—No sin). The middle self must learn to live and work with others (Serve to Deserve). And the Higher Self must advance to the point of loving and unselfish service to others. In determining your own future, it is best to include it within the wider world future, picturing peace and betterment for yourself, family, friends, and the world. This is ecological.

When it comes to changes in your future which involve others, you must take care not to impose your will on others. The Kahuna taught that the minding of one's own business was most important, and to ask anything that would be hurtful to another person would be to set his Higher Self against you.

In trying to decide what you wish your future to be, begin by asking and inviting your High Self to give you guidance and take a hand in your life. Then display the good sense to listen and the discipline to act upon what your High Self tells you.

LESSON 7: REVIEW AND INSPIRATION

Most important, there IS a life force that exists. The Polynesian Kahuna called it Mana. In addition, many other terms have been used to describe this life force. Paracelsus (1490-1541) called it "mumia." The medieval alchemists called it "vital fluid." Dr. Oscar Brunler called it "bio-cosmic energy." The healing power of Jesus referred to it as "virtue." The Kabbalists named it "Astral Light." In the Pali language, it is "Eckankar." And various cultural groups have had specific names for this life force: "Prana," by the ancient Hindus; "ka," by the Egyptians; "chi," by the Chinese; "ki," by the Japanese, "El," by the Hebrews; and "ambrosia," by the Greeks in their mythology (Wingo, 1973, No. 7, p. 3). Even the popular movie, "Star Wars," had a name for it: The Force.

Huna teaches that this force can be increased and used for specific purposes. This can be done through the breath or by a firm mental command without any sort of breathing exercise.

Long quotes from a famous treatise called "Light on the Path" to inspire students of Huna. It is set forth in aphorisms, from which he quotes the pertinent ones:

17. Seek out the way.

18. Seek the way by retreating within.

19. *Seek the way by advancing boldly without.*

20. *SEEK IT NOT BY ANY ONE ROAD. To each temperament, there is one road which seems the most desirable. But the way is not found by devotion alone, by religious contemplation alone, by ardent progress, by self-sacrificing labor, by studious observation of life. None alone can take the disciple more than one step onwards. All steps are necessary to make up the ladder... The whole nature of man must be used wisely by the one who desires to enter the way. Each man is to himself absolutely the way, the truth, and life. But he is only so when he grasps his whole individuality firmly, and, by the force of his awakened spiritual will, recognizes this individuality as not himself, but that thing which he has with pain created for his own use, and by means of which he purposes, as his growth slowly develops his intelligence, to reach to the life beyond individuality. When he knows that for this his wonderful complex, separated life exists, then, indeed, and then only, he is upon the way. Seek it by plunging into the mysterious and glorious depths of your own inmost being. Seek it by testing all experience, by utilizing the senses, in order to understand the growth and meaning of individuality, and the beauty and obscurity of those other divine fragments which are struggling side by side with you, and form the race to which you belong. Seek it by study of the laws of being, the laws of nature, the laws of the supernatural; and seek it by making the profound obeisance of the soul to the dim star that burns within. Steadily, as you watch and worship, its light will grow stronger. Then you may know you have found the beginning of the way. And, when you have found the end, its light*

will suddenly become the infinite light. (Wingo, 1973, No. 7, p. 5.)

Look within yourself for the truth, and when you look, see that you have three levels of consciousness (three selves) and that the discovery of the low self is important, but *the recognition of the High Self is the secret of Huna.* Look always for the unity of the three selves working together in harmony for the good of all. Learn how to make the thought forms of desired results and send them in the prayer-action to the High Self. Learn the faith to know they will come about by the continual repetition of the work. Learn these lessons on the intellectual level of understanding and also on the low self level of actual acceptance.

LESSON 8: CLEARING THE PATH

Let us discuss the clearing of the path of the obstructions that can block your prayer-action from being completed and prevent contact from being made between the low self and the High Self. This has to do with the preparation ritual known as "kala," or "cleansing," the clearing of the path.

Feelings of guilt can cause the low self to believe that one has sinned and does not deserve to have one's prayers answered. Huna recognizes the only "sin" as that of hurting another. The "kala," or cleansing which is a forgiveness or restoration of the symbolic light, *is effective only when the low self can be convinced that amends have been made.* Amends must be made for wrongs which one has done. In the cases where amends can be made directly to the person wronged, this is done. In cases where this is not possible, the low self is impressed by the doing of good deeds to others.

It was the low self who did the wrong in the first place, although it was the middle self that judged it as wrong. Therefore, the low self must right the wrong and the middle self must let go of the idea that a wrong has been done.

One can also feel guilty for doing something which actually caused no harm to another person. This results from fixations which are held by the low self. Remember, the low self is the conscience, *after* it receives orders from the middle self as to what is right and wrong. As a result of *misunderstood* experiences, the low self may hold on to beliefs which are mistaken ideas of its guilt in regard to certain supposed wrongs. These beliefs are not logical, since the low self has only deductive reasoning; however, the low self still feels guilty. So the clearing of the path becomes a personal matter, for what it boils down to is this:

> *Whatever you have been taught and have come to believe is wrong (usually on the low self sense level, but it may also include the middle self conscious reasoning level), THAT IS A SIN TO YOU, and how strongly fixed the guilt feeling is in the low self and the degree of intensity of the emotional reaction to it— these are individual matters and depend entirely upon your experiences in life.*
>
> *Anything that keeps your low self from acting to make contact with your High Self and delivering the prayer picture along the aka-cord breaks up the team of three selves (Wingo, 1973, No. 8, p. 7).*

All fixations are based upon what might be called renegade memories. Here is where you must check out your own reactions to all of your own renegade memories. Long recommends the "Twinge" or "nanao" method. The word "na-na-o" means to "think deeply; to penetrate, as into the mind, to thrust the hand into some unknown and dark receptacle to search for something." The thing that is sought after is the fixation, so the mind may be quieted.

To do this, one sits as if in meditation; however, with a particular goal in mind. Give the low self the firm command, "Go search into all your store of memories for those times when I was under emotional stress such as anger, fear, shock, etc."

Look for and notice that strange little indication in the pit of the stomach, a sort of sinking feeling or a mini-replay of the reaction experienced at the time. Go back and deal with all these experiences and neutralize them so they no longer hold any power over the low self. Go over anything that might give you a clue to a fixation. As you do this surround yourself in Huna Light.

LESSON 9: KALA CLEANSING

As you are checking yourself for emotional reactions, it is important to bear in mind that there are also the positive emotions, such as love and joy. These are important emotions that help the low self to do its work, and we are not looking to clear these out. We need these in order to live a life of joy and eagerness. We are looking only for the emotions which are *negative in the sense they block the path from the low self to the High Self.*

As you are doing this, you will confront old patterns of belief and thought. Huna does not ask that you change any of these beliefs which may provide inspiration and courage to you in your daily living, but rather that you sort out dogma from unquestioned authorities in your past. As we grow, we learn first parental law, then we come into contact with natural law, and finally we begin to see that there are cosmic laws governing us all. We are aiming to get more in tune with these cosmic laws. Reading inspirational literature will help at this time.

There is no specific ritual which is necessary, but anything that will help your low self to get the message will be helpful. Remember, prayer is not a "thinking" alone. It is a combination of thinking and a gesture or physical movement of the low self by which it creates mana and gives it to the High Self. Fasting can at times help to get the attention of the low self, but it does not work for everyone.

Remember, getting rid of guilt is the process of going back and undoing the hurt. It can be done. It is also important to forgive others who have harmed us. We need to forgive others, for *as long as we are holding a grudge and hate someone, the low self will not be able to get through to the High Self.*

LESSON 10: CREATING THOUGHT FORMS

Let us discuss the making of the thought forms to match the picture of what is sought in prayer. It is by means of these thought-forms that the low self presents to the High Self that the idea is brought into reality. For this reason, *the High Self needs a very clear and consistent picture of what is desired,* or it will become confused and not know what it is we want created.

Remember, we always have free will; the High Self does not impose its will upon us, but depends upon us to tell it what we want so that it can help us with our desires. First we need to decide definitely what it is we want. Then we need to inspect all the parts of that decision and clarify the outline. In doing so, we must remember not to encroach upon the rights of another. As we are working out this description in words, we are beginning to *draw a mental picture of the desired situation.* This is called visualization, which is thinking in pictures as well as words. Imagine yourself in the desired situation, enjoying the benefits of what you hope to obtain. Remember, the clearer the picture, the more exact will be the results.

In many cases you should not decide exactly HOW the High Self will bring your picture into reality, but give it to the High Self with trust and confidence that it will do so. However, this does not mean to try to convince yourself that you ALREADY have the desired result. It is more a question of faith that it will happen. Remember, you will be creating a mold of new conditions in "aka" substance. The old molds will have to be torn down first, and this will take some time and patience on your part. Don't expect too much too soon. We reap what we sow. Prepare the ground, plant the seed, water it daily, forget about the seed, and then reap the harvest.

LESSON 11: THREE SELF UNITY

There are the three selves, and any attempt to suppress any one of them results in an unbalanced, abnormal life. Some advocate a completely "spiritual" life, denying that there is any good in the "worldly" things. Others seek out all the material and physical pleasures without any regard for the spiritual. Both of these are extreme positions.

Our life is harmonious when all three selves are working together, doing their part, for the good of the whole. The Kahuna taught that man had been given endless joys as well as some sorrows, that life was good and beautiful when lived normally. Growth and experiences were normal and necessary for life. The fact that the High Self is standing with, in, and above us as a spirit and representative of Universal Spirit gives us the power and ability to contact this great being for protection and help. We do not need to struggle.

LESSON 12: GUIDANCE

The harmonious working together of the three selves is our goal. Yet even with this common purpose, the process of Huna is a very individual thing. Seek the help and guidance of the High Self, yet do not minimize the part of either the low self or the middle self. They both have important parts to play in the functioning of the individual. When it becomes a regular and natural part of your daily life, your life will be in harmony and balance.

As you recognize guidance from your High Self, you will grow into Light and be thereby enabled to see the Path. How can you tell that you are in contact with the High Self? The answer, which is never satisfactory to those who ask, is that until you have experienced it, you will not know. It comes as a kind of "knowing," or "awareness," or "realization." You will have to learn to distinguish the source of the inner voice. It comes as a bit of intuition, a hunch, or a set of circumstances. Sometimes it is not recognized until much later; that is why it is important to seek continuous guidance from the High Self level. You will need to develop patience and an attitude of watchful waiting. Seek guidance, keep an open mind, stay alert and expectant. The flashes of guidance will come.

This basic course in Huna, compiled by Otha Wingo according to the concepts Max Freedom Long put forth, was designed to give the reader an idea of how Long believed the system of the Kahuna worked. He devoted his life to unlocking the secrets, and now they are available to everyone. They are based on logic and reason, and they do work when applied correctly.

They include Long's version of the flow of energy, both healing and harmful, and sin as a source of disruption that harms the person. The aim of the Kahuna is to correct this flow of energy within himself or herself and then through ritual and meditation to correct the disrupted flow in the sufferer. The balanced relation of the three selves plays an important role in this process.

In the next chapter we will look at the work of David Kaonohiokala Bray, who has presented this material to Westerners and Hawaiians from a Hawaiian perspective. Then we shall look at some of the similarities and differences between the teachings of Long and Bray.

CHAPTER 4

DAVID KAONOHIOKALA BRAY: HIS LIFE AND WORK

"To the Hawaiian there are two great forces, the Higher and the Lower."

David Kaonohiokala Bray was born in March, 1889, and passed on in November, 1968. He was an initiated Hawaiian priest and the last of the publicly practicing Kahuna. He descended from a family of "Po'o" (head) Kahuna. His family served the kings of the Island of Hawaii for twenty-five generations. He tells the story in his own words:

I am the fifth generation from the High Priest Holoae who was with Kamehameha the Conqueror at the Battle of Mokuokai which began Kamehameha's career. Holoae cast the auguries and interpreted the omens at the beginning of the battle... My own family stems from Namahana, daughter of Holoae. I was adopted as a baby by my Aunt Luika and reared in a house next door to Great Aunt Kailianu. Mama Luika was a Kahuna and I learned from both of them... I think I was destined to be a Kahuna... Mama Luika wisely said that I must conquer my temper and prove that I had the god of light within me (Bray and Low, 1980, p. 3).

Bray says that Kahuna are priests and priestesses, spiritual teachers. They act as bridges between the spiritual world and its laws and the material world with its problems, trials and sadnesses. It is important for the Kahuna to be in harmony with nature as well as himself. Once he has achieved harmony within himself, his character becomes calm and dignified. As a result, he gains the trust of the gods to keep the secrets of nature while using the wisdom in helping mankind. While some Kahuna gave in to the temptations of power and jealousy, they were the rare exceptions. The majority used the secrets of nature to serve humanity for goodness and truth.

Of his training, Bray says:

"To be a Kahuna, a person is taught all about the material things of life, the negative part. He has to know what harmony and unity is within himself, God, and mankind.

"He must live according to the secret meaning of Aloha:

A, 'ala,' watchful alertness

L, 'lokahi,' working with unity

O, 'oiaio,' truthful honesty

H, 'ha'aha'a,' humility

A, 'ahonui,' patient perseverance.

"Kahuna had to learn these things. When they learned them, they found God. Then they beheld nature as God created it...

"The Kahuna learned from the beginning to be fearless and overcome doubt. Fear causes emotional confusion. Doubt causes emotional confusion. When the

*mind is confused we say that matter controls mind...
Fear and doubt create false gods. The forces of dark-
ness surround you and come to dwell in you. Kahuna
teach freedom from Satan, whom Hawaiians call
"Milu," by conquering fear and doubt." (Bray and
Low, 1980, p. 2)*

Bray talked a lot about the dark forces. He believed,
as he was taught, that they do exist and man needs to be
aware of them in order to remain free and clear of their
evil ways. Only by understanding and examining his true
nature could a person overcome these forces, rather than
being overcome by them. As a person delved into his
emotions, he found out all the hideous parts of himself
that had to be reconciled. Bray was quick to point out that
the dark forces, which manifested themselves as negative
emotions such as hate, fear, anger, envy, and greed, are a
part of a person, rather than the person being a part of
these dark forces. In other words, if a person is filled with
hate, hate is a part of the person, rather than the person
being a part of the hate. In this way the hate could be cut
off, and in its place could be put love, unselfishness, trust,
courage, as the case may be.

Bray believed in learning through experience. It was
very important to him. He used a particular phrase to
describe each person's experiences and knowledge that
made him unique. He called it a person's "calabash of
knowledge." He felt one should learn through his experiences, taking what fit and giving back the rest. He felt all
people were equal, and because of this, he was willing and
eager to teach the non-Hawaiian even if it meant risking
ridicule from the Hawaiians who did not understand what
he was doing. He felt we always have the choice of whose
side we want to be on: the forces of darkness or the forces
of light. The choice is always ours, and we have to be
aware of this.

The important thing to a Kahuna starting out is to

know who he/she is and to make the foundation of his/her faith strong. Faith is required, but faith without understanding is nothing, so one needs to study and examine things in order to understand. This understanding involves the concept of balance within and without as well.

The particular kind of Kahuna that Bray was, "Po'o-Kahuna," was familiar with every phase of Kahuna learning. "Po'o-Kahuna" had the power to heal through prayer and faith. They had the power to prophesy and to interpret omens.

Only those who had the gift of the gods were trained in the priesthood. The priests could recognize this gift in a newborn child, and such a child received training from an early age. A person had to have what the Hawaiians call "ike," spiritual power, which can be transmitted to others. "Ike" is the force which Bray said gave the ability to heal through faith. At death, a Kahuna passes on his or her spiritual powers to a chosen one, usually a son or daughter or grandson or granddaughter.

Bray also was given sacred feathers and a sacred stone which contained spiritual power which he used. The power in these objects is in the consciousness they evoke. In the case of spiritually powerful objects, they were able to evoke a high spiritual consciousness.

The central focus for Bray was definitely spiritual and the function of different spiritual forces. While Long emphasized only the existence of the good forces, Bray's approach, which is probably closer to the Hawaiian tradition, emphasizes the existence of both beneficial and harmful forces. He also emphasizes the notion of spiritual life or force, much more than Long did.

Bray believed that all things on earth received a certain amount of spiritual life from the divine powers which lived "beyond the clouds." This spiritual life is called "mana." Mana can be received from heaven and be passed on to do supernatural deeds or to perform healing or good deeds. A rock or a tree can have "mana," just as human

beings can.
Bray says:

> *Mana was received from heaven through prayer. A man prayed constantly and made daily offerings to his own Aumakua, a spiritual guardian spirit, generally an ancestor. The Aumakua, being in heaven, listened to his child on earth and interceded with the great god for this divine spirit. It was as though heaven were a reservoir of spiritual power and that power descended to the Kahuna on earth through the Aumakua. The more the Kahuna prayed, the more spiritual power he received, until his person was like a small reservoir of spiritual power (Bray and Low, 1980, p. 10).*

The real spiritual strength of the Hawaiian lies in his belief in aumakua, spiritual ancestors who live in the heavens, the sun, the moon, and the stars. The Hawaiian believes his aumakua takes a personal interest in his life, visiting him in dreams and giving him help in all his troubles.

Bray felt that the evil work done by a Kahuna ana-ana, or sorcerer, can hit back and kill the sorcerer, while the one cursed can rise above the evil. The evil is done by the sorcerer in undermining the character of the person cursed. A strong person cannot be affected by the curse of a sorcerer; it is only the weak or inexperienced who are affected. The sorcerer creates hate in the mind of a weak person and gives the cursed one a lifelong alibi for his faults or weaknesses. The weak person is always able to use the curse as justification for his weak or bad behavior. Such a person would need to be taught to blame his faults on himself and rid himself of hate in order to better himself.

Bray was a Christian and found no difficulty in being one within his Kahuna tradition. He felt at the same time that the Hawaiians who became Christians needed to declare their purpose to their family aumakua in a ceremony, before starting out on a new path of light. He felt the aumakua were only interested in the highest and best for their earthly children and would support them. However, they were like all parents, and wanted to be consulted and remembered. In all of Bray's teaching, faith was the strongest element.

The Hawaiians did not fear God, they loved Him. To them, fear is unreality and to serve God with fear is not to serve Him at all but to become selfish and weak. We do not teach our children to fear us. We teach them to love us so that they will have confidence in us when we try to help them. In the same way the Hawaiians loved God and had confidence in Him. The spiritual comes into the material world when there is love and confidence.

Both Christ and the Kahuna taught that the kingdom of Heaven is within us. What does this mean? Within us are both the Spirit and Matter. Bray felt that the most important thing that the world can learn from the Kahuna is the lesson of combining the spiritual and the material. We must know them both.

This is the secret of the Kahuna. We have to reflect the light of God and stop fearing the darkness. Turn toward the light and go within. Even if a person is weak, he can be sincere in his effort to destroy fear. If he is sincere, God will send him help and give him strength and destroy the dark forces. Then confidence will replace doubt and love will replace fear.

To combine the spiritual and material, one cannot deny either. Some people are only materialistic; others are only spiritual. Life is a combination, and to know ourselves we must know both parts of nature. Hawaiians have always loved the joys of nature and materialistic pleasures, but happiness has never kept them from loving God.

The material and spiritual go together. The person

who balances these two forces has a strong foundation. He succeeds in life. When you understand that your real self is the God in your heart, there is no obstacle to your success. This is because we are all part of God. To understand God is to know that part of God that is within us.

Bray says:

> *What are the parts in us we must understand? The material is the negative part. It is what we crave for and the desire for earthly things. We have to be honest and admit what we desire. But we will also know what is good for us and what is bad. When we know something will hurt either ourselves or other people, but do it anyway, we become weak. We call it his or her weakness. The spiritual part is the law of love. God's law is unity and harmony. This is the positive part in us that creates brotherhood.*
>
> *When we bring the positive part of unity and harmony and love into the negative part, then we will have the truth. Personal craving is the negative. God's law is the positive. When we know how to bring personal craving and love together, there is Light. God shines in us and we enjoy true happiness (Bray and Low, 1980, p. 24).*

Bray wanted to teach people how to protect themselves and to help other people with their problems. One of the ways he did this best was to talk to people and share with them stories about himself and other people he knew. From a dream he was guided to go to a certain store and buy a stone and have it set to wear as a ring to help others in healing. He used a lot of jewelry, which he loved, in healing.

He was joined in "spiritual contact" with certain other people who shared the same aumakua. They knew when another was in trouble, and the agreement was that they

would then come and help. He listened to the inner voice
and was true to it. He had the wisdom and discipline to
follow it.

As a child, Bray was not taught about reincarnation.
He was taught that when you die you go to the other side
and maybe if you are a good person they send you back to
be a guide to another person and see that he is not in
trouble. However, in his later life he began to have experiences which made him more receptive to the theory of
reincarnation. As he grew older, it was a subject that
increasingly fascinated him. More and more he began to
delve into it. He met a man from India with whom he
shared a close link and deep spiritual bond. The man told
him they had been brothers in a previous life. By the end
of his life, Bray was certainly leaning toward the belief in
reincarnation, but was searching for proof. He felt that if
he could only prove reincarnation, then it would not matter what anyone said about it.

Since his death his views have changed, according to
Eileen Charlton, a healer and trance medium in a holistic
medical clinic at Cedars Sinai Medical Towers in Los
Angeles. In June, 1981, she wrote an article for the Huna
Vistas Newsletter in which she communicated information from Bray. Bray now says that the Hawaiians of old
believed in reincarnation.

Perhaps for Long the source of spiritual power seemed
to come more from knowledge, which is more typical of
Western spirituality. For Bray, there existed definite
ways of tapping into and increasing spiritual power. This
personal spiritual power was increased through a person's
efforts more than through the acquisition of knowledge.
One of the methods used to increase spiritual power is
meditation.

Bray believed in meditation. He felt it was important
to be able to clear the mind from outside distractions and
to clear the imagination of the rubbish of fantasy. No real
work can be done by the Kahuna unless his mind is free

and clear. He establishes contact with his Aumakua(s) with a free and clear mind. He examines his own emotions. There are positive emotions which lift us up and there are negative emotions which pull us down. The point is not to strive to become emotionless, but to use the positive ones.

The Kahuna draws on the universal energy and psychic forces in order to see the spiritual forces and diagnose the problem by their help. But he cannot do this until his mind is free from outside distractions and clear of the rubbish of the imagination. This is done through meditation.

There are three steps to right meditation:

1. *Relax the body, mind, and emotions. The body must be able to let loose of all tension and be free from any pain that might interfere with a free mind. Also, the mind must be relaxed so that it can be open to psychic impressions. If the mind is tense, then it cannot focus on the next two steps. Just as important as the relaxation of the body and mind is the relaxation of the emotions. The Kahuna must not work if he is filled with negative emotions. If he is envious, hateful, or emotionally disturbed, then the mind cannot become free and clear. He will also attract negative spirits of the lowest kind, who will serve him only to trap him later. Relaxation of the body, mind, and emotions is the first step.*

2. *Empty the mind completely. All images, thoughts, and elements of the imagination must be discarded. When the mind is empty, then it will seem that the head is filled with light. This is kukui or the psychic energy. Kahuna believe that the psychic light enters the body and fills the inner cavern or haven of the spirit in between the eyes (lua Uhane). Unless the mind is completely*

emptied the light cannot flow in and there will be obstacles and distortions in meditation.

3.   *Focus the consciousness on the purpose of the meditation. If it is a problem, focus the mind on the problem as if God and the spirits who watch over the welfare of man were solving it. Feel that the problem is already solved and be receptive to the solution. If you are working for someone, see that person in the haven of the spirit or lua Uhane. See the person in your mind's eye, in the light that flows into you. See the person as perfect.*

This method of meditation is used in preparing the mind to address God in prayer and the aumakua through chants.   Each step is important, and the Kahuna uses everything that helps him so he is open to inspiration that will lead to help.

To get rid of the negative, we get above them, higher than they are, and then simply throw them out. We fill up with light.

To the Hawaiian there are two great forces, the higher and the lower. We go from the darkness to the light. Focus your mind so you can see from the inside. See with your inner eye. This is where the positive is and where the power comes in. If you are negative, the positive shrinks and you become negative. Concentrate on the positive, shrink the negative and become positive (Bray, 1963a).

Bray taught that God is form and without form. Without form He is the great presence, and with form He is the four elements: air, fire, water, earth. Man grows out of the four elements.   They produce man.   To the Hawaiians, man is part of nature.

You may choose your own guides and masters, but do

not disregard the guides and masters of others. It is also important to acknowledge all of your ancestors who have been approved by the great power.

In Bray's teaching the supreme God is "I'O" or "IAO", the I AM presence. Aumakua (which has up to this point been defined as: high self, god-self, super conscious mind) is not the same as Bray's use of aumakua (lower case "a") which is a general term for gods, goddesses, and high spirits from beyond this world. Some are concerned with the development of this world. The highest ones can work as intermediaries to the High Forces who never contact this world. There are two types: highest and lowest. The lower spirits are of this world, earth bound. They are negative or positive. Each Kahuna has its own special spirits to be contacted.

The rituals and prayers are designed to contact the aumakua. These aumakua are descended from aumakua who lived on this world a long time ago. The highest aumakua are Kane, creator; Ku, destroyer; Kanaloa, sustainer; and Lono, the messenger of the gods to man. In order to contact the great power, we go through intermediaries rather than doing so directly, but it must be kept in mind that *we only worship the Supreme God and do not make gods out of the aumakua.*

As we have seen, meditation was very important to Bray. It was the method used by the Kahuna for preparing the mind for addressing the Aumakua (high self, god-self, super conscious mind), and the aumakua (a general term for spirits and or gods, usually helpful) by prayer and chant. First, one relaxed. Second, one freed the mind from emotional distractions. Third, one focused the mind upon the object of prayer. The chants which were used to invoke the Aumakua derived their power from the cosmic forces. Lono is the power of heaven. The power that arises within the sincere person who has made himself worthy of addressing the aumakua is the result of coming into harmony with the great forces of nature outside himself that are also present within him. This inner force is the same as the energy of nature, the mana, the "ike." These forces are localized in the human body in certain areas.

Bray described true prayer by saying that true prayer must be sincere. With doubt or pretense, the power will not be released, and you will fail. Prayer must also be spontaneous. As one meditates, he tunes into the aumakua. Prayer must not be just the expression of the little self. In prayer we reach beyond the limited self into the infinite mind of God. Prayer is simple and childlike. It comes from the sincere heart which states simply its feelings and needs. Man is the child of the gods, so trust is the real way to talk with the aumakua. Talk from the inside about what you really want.

The special chants have definite words, and the master Kahuna are taught to use special tones and gestures, but within the heart of the Kahuna must be sincerity, spontaneity, sensitivity, lack of selfishness, harmony with the great power of nature, and a childlike simplicity. Ritual does not get in the way of simplicity and sincerity.

Bray says:

The chants act as a bridge between the Kahuna and the aumakua. Practicing the chants develops the qualities of the Kahuna. Often more takes place on the psychic and spiritual level than is apparent on the physical as the result of prayer and chanting. As one goes along one increases spiritually (Bray, 1964).

Bray advised one to take time and not hurry. He said that we are not working for ourselves but for the great power, and should remember to be thankful for the light we have.

Bray believed doubt is fear. When one doubts, one fears, and becomes confused and depressed. We fear because we do not understand our real self and the real God. God is a loving God. We have to know who we are, to make the foundation strong. That is why Bray said a Kahuna may teach you everything about your negative side. We have to be balanced, set our foundations, and understand the meaning of balance. We have to understand, because faith without understanding is nothing. To pray without understanding means nothing.

No one can lead you to God; they can only show you the way. Keep your vibrations clear, and protect yourself from the dark forces by staying alert. Honor the teachings of others *but never accept anything you do not want for yourself,* and pray for one another and for increased mutual understanding which will bring spiritual understanding.

Bray recognized a form of energy, as Long did, that is the basis of the universe. He set down principles that deal with the basic pattern by which all energy manifests in form. He believed everything is a manifestation of divine energy.

Bray is sometimes difficult to understand with the mind because he has to be experienced by the senses and the emotions as well as the intellect. I experienced Bray's spirit directly on a trip I made to Kona, a spot on the Big Island of Hawaii, which is his ancestral home. He came to me and passed on some information about energy and the chakras, and then he asked me to remain in Kona rather than return to San Diego. I blessed him, thanked him for the information and help, but told him I would be returning to San Diego as planned.

Through this experience I learned from Bray on an intuitive level, which is hard to put into words because it was a very personal experience. After weeks and months of listening to tapes of his teachings and of reading material he had written, I experienced his energy first hand. I experienced a very loving but very forceful man who wanted to have his way. He was very convincing and promised me a lot. However, when I turned him down, he did not turn his back on me. Rather, he admired me more for knowing my own mind and following my inner voice that was giving me guidance.

Three days later on the plane back to San Diego I again felt Bray with me, this time as a more peaceful companion. I felt him helping me across the bridge from the spirit world as I helped him across from the material world. I learned that the one cannot exist without the other. They are not exclusive of one another. They are complementary.

Bray was a Kahuna of the order of Kane. Serge King, in his book *Kahuna Healing* (1979), talks about the order of Kane. This approach is a spiritual and integrative approach, as compared to a sensual and emotional approach (the order of Ku), or an intellectual and mechanical approach (the order of Lono). In the order of Kane, the world is approached as merely a reflection of our thought. There is emphasis on unification or integration of body, mind, and spirit for the purpose of self-mastery. Self-mastery is believed to be the key to mastery of life.

In healing, the importance is put on thought. Presently held beliefs are believed to be more important than past experiences. Imagination is an important tool. The Kahuna in the order of Kane are pragmatic philosophers who work with alternate states of consciousness and refined use of psychic abilities. All these descriptions fit Bray.

Bray wrote concerning the origin of human destiny and the keepers of the sacred secret. The principles deal with the manifestation of energy according to the use of the sacred name of God of the Hawaiians. This name was said aloud by only one priest in any given generation and held very sacred. The name was unknown to the commoner.

The basic pattern by which all energy manifests in form contains clues as to what humanity is supposed to learn on this planet, how that human destiny is related to the universe as a whole, and what the responsibilities of the initiatory line of priests have been from the beginning. The principles offer a unique interpretation. The language is deliberately technical and hard to understand and grasp on casual reading. This is to force the reader to use the principles as foci for meditation and deep contemplation. The order of the principles is important, and so the paragraphs are numbered and each one interrelates to the previous paragraphs.

A casual, intellectual understanding will not reveal the deep implications of the meaning. They are principles compiled over generations and require careful study and concentration as well as application in order to understand. Here is a summary of Bray's principles:

1. *Everything is a manifestation of divine energy.*

2. *Divine energy is neither self-existent nor self-created. It depends upon the mysterious source symbolized by the Hawaiians in the name I-A-O. "I" means the creative act by which that which is perfect manifests the creator who is imperfect and can only create that which is perfect.*

3. *"A" means the radiation of divine energy as the universe of multidimensions. The four-dimensional world as we know it is basically space and time. The pattern of life and form does not arise from this world as we know it. This is true of the extensions of space and time we experience in imagination, dreams, psychic states, and in the after-death state.*

4. *The great power of space/time, we call the sun. From across eternity and out of another dimension came humanity to be linked up with this great power called the sun. Along with humanity came all who care for humanity and those for whom humanity is responsible. We came as individuals, and yet all manifestations*

of one power, as if in the form of sparks of light.

5.   *Our planet was formed by the Sun to be our home. Forms arose which could house the sparks of life. However, humanity required a special act. So Guardian Spirits who are beyond Solar development came with us across Po, Eternal Night. Some of those sparks willed to take on temporary physical form in order to create the human race. This is the origin of our dual nature: one connected with material form and one connected with pure spirit.*

6.   *The Guardian Spirits taught humanity the true destiny of life, which is also twofold: We are to enjoy the beauty of nature, and we are to realize consciously our spiritual nature through mutual love.*

7.   *All the other forms of life on this planet have Guardian Spirits as well, and we should recognize them and learn to live in harmony with them.*

8.   *Spirits outside our Solar evolution visit us from time to time. They are our friends and we have no business challenging them.*

9.   *The Guardian Spirits showed humanity how to live happily, healthily, and advance spiritually. After having done this, most of the Guardian spirits departed again as divine sparks. Some remained without material forms; and some few blended to form the true priesthoods of the ancient religions. These latter established lines of descent, for they were not and could not be materially immortal.*

10. *After many eras the "O" function of the Sacred Name began to operate. If humanity can make*

reality out of divine power, so can it experience unreality. Unreality is mis-perception and misinterpretation, which lead to negative emotions and wrong actions, and these in turn lead to unhappiness, illness, and death.

11. *In terms of humanity's dual nature, this is why we must consider both sides of man's nature. When we turn to spirit alone, we miss the beauty of nature. When we turn to material form alone, we lose the life of love.*

12. *Humanity fell away from the balanced teaching and sought power through matter. Nature, when abused, ceases to be beautiful, and humanity, along with all life forms, suffers.*

13. *Those who return to the instructions and teachings of the Guardian Spirits who first came to teach us can restore humanity to its balance. Those who do not will be temporarily destroyed.*

14. *The method of return to the teachings and balance is selfless service, which alone truly allows joy in the beauty of nature to combine with mutual love. This was the way of the real Kahuna of Hawaii.*

15. *Such a person is fit to understand and utter the Sacred Name, I-A-O.*

After Bray discussed the origin of human destiny and the keepers of the sacred secret, he went on to outline the Guardian Spirits themselves and the law of polarity. In doing so he used the terms body, soul, and spirit to express the aspects of reality interacting together in the realms of nature. By body he meant the basic life forms and their energies. He included what is often called matter, ethereal force, and astral emotionality, as well as all gross elements and vegetative/animal awareness.

Soul includes higher emotional aspiration and mental awareness bordering on spiritual intuition. Soul works through intelligence and will to create forms of expression on the bodily plane.

Spirit is the plane of pure being as energy rather than form. It is undifferentiated contact with God and the supreme power of Mana.

We live on all three planes. However, most of humanity is caught in the illusory trap that consciousness centers on the first plane of body with perhaps flashes of insight into the soul level. Advanced people recognize the limits of body and center their aspirations in soul because they have flashes of insight into the spirit plane.

Within bodily understanding we view our relation to God as servitude; with soul understanding we realize that we are part of God through love; with the understanding of the spirit we are divine. It is important to distinguish the enthusiasm of insight and the emotions it releases from true spiritual achievements. The first is illusory and transient; the second is permanent.

On the bodily plane we perceive through the senses in limited time and space, conditioned by the past (memory) and the future (anticipation). The result is ignorance, egoism, frustration, and the experience of pleasure and pain. On the soul plane we feel and think in extended space and time, gaining knowledge, true individuality, hope, and illuminated ecstasy. On the spiritual plane, all space is here and all time is now. There is nothing to gain and nothing to experience. This is the plane of realization.

Bodily consciousness works through the separation or division of subject and object. They are connected by the processes of knowing and activity and are motivated by desire. Subject-desire-object or subject-action-object or knower-knowing-known are all methods which operate on this level.

Soul consciousness recognizes the union of subject

and object rather than seeing them as separate. As a unity they produce experience: subject/object producing perception, knower/known producing perception, or subject/action producing perception. Desire still plays a role, but it is no longer a desire for an externalized object by an internalized subject. Inner and outer are no longer meaningful. Spiritual consciousness makes knower, knowing, and known one, so that perception, knowledge, and action occur simultaneously. This is because they have no need to be differentiated. Desire no longer has any presence whatever. There is pure freedom and completeness.

To operate from the body to the soul to the spirit is the lesson of life. To operate from the spirit to the soul to the body is Kahuna mastery.

16. *All manifestation functions in terms of polarity and periodicity. Polarity divides the one energy into a dynamic dualism of interaction. Periodicity arranges the modes of interaction into an orderly hierarchy.*

17. *All energy transformations in nature require both intelligence and will. Intelligence directs the pattern of exchange from one aspect of energy to another; will directs the direction and use of exchange.*

18. *Form is energy in a spiral pattern of cyclic activity. The pattern may be more or less stable. However, energy flows constantly into and out of that spiral, or in some cases interwoven spirals, from the universal source of the great power into the individual form.*

19. *Energy changes affecting form, act in a hierarchy directly proportional to the level of intelligence and amount of will involved. All life forms belong to this hierarchy, and those with non-*

*material bodies (according to our senses) who
guide and guard other life forms are called
aumakua by the Polynesians.*

20. *Those Guardian Spirits acting on mental and
lower forms can make their presence known by
(a) moving objects in unusual fashions, (b)
stimulating changes in perceptions through
acting on our energy fields or auras, or (c)
temporarily taking objects as centers of
concentration or "homes," as in the case of
amulets, talismen, fetishes, ritual objects and
meditational images. These may be manmade or
naturally formed. The Guardian Spirits may
also temporarily act through another life form.*

21. *All life expressions remain forever linked with
each other as to the Universal Oversoul. Creative
Kahuna work must be related to the totality.
Abuse of Kahuna power relies on the illusion of
separation. The Kahuna learns the plan of God
through self-knowledge, which is meditation, and
experience, which is ritual.*

22. *Those intelligences in the hierarchy who
influence the perceptions through manipulation
of the aura produce phenomena rarely subject to
instrumental verification. Thus the aumakua act
both directly on a subjective level and objectively
when using an embodied life form. There need be
no controversy among materialistic, psychic, and
psychological interpretations of Kahuna activity.
All three interpretations act as one.*

23. *Aumakua may be divided into the following
groups: (a) those beyond our planetary evolution.
(b) those linked with it but complete masters over
it, who thus act only indirectly; (c) those
concerned with non-human activities of nature;*

(d) those concerned with humanity as a whole; (e) those concerned with special groups and epochs; (f) those concerned with special family lines; (g) those concerned with priestly, initiatory orders; (h) those concerned with special individuals; (i) those whose functions overlap two or more of these categories; and (j) those who are achieving the goal of becoming true Servant and Guardian spirits.

24. *Among the groups from (c) through (i) above, there may be found the following subdivisions: (a) those who are of the highest energy and are free from earthly influences, (b) those who are partially free but influenced by earthly powers and their elements, (c) those who are as powerful as the highest but whose destiny makes them earthbound, (d) those whose powers are limited to our planetary elements and are earthbound, and (e) those who take on the appearance of any of the first four but whose nature is demonic and whose motivation is deception.*

25. *For meditational and ritual purposes, each of the aumakua are connected with the universal energy in terms of the traditional elements: AIR, those who are free from earthly forces; FIRE, those who transform energy forms freely; WATER, those who nourish and defend; EARTH, those who stabilize. Many other symbols are connected with each aumakua. These are taught through initiation and direct contact.*

26. *A developed person may serve as a bridge between the dual modes of expression in matter / spirit, activity / passivity, life flow / life withdrawal, evolution / destruction, etc. To do this, he or she must establish contact with all appropriate members of the hierarchy of*

Guardian Spirits appropriate for the work with which he or she wishes to cooperate.

27. *The teachings and initial mana for preparation are given freely by an initiate of the traditional priestly line, once the person has proven himself or herself worthy. Further progress involves applying the teachings to principle number 25. The work is therefore accomplished by a combination of meditation and ritual.*

28. *Cooperation among similarly developed individuals strengthens the results of the work.*

29. *The first necessity is for the person to integrate and allow to flow harmoniously the polarities of mind and emotion, then spirit and body. This is begun by not seeking power, but by discovering the psychological roots for our positive and negative psychological characteristics. Meeting this first necessity is the only sure way of aligning the true self with the Great Power, and therefore the aumakua, who serve God. This is also the only sure path away from illusion to reality, from fear to love, and from bondage to service.*

30. *The reason why the conditions of principles numbers 26 through 29 must be met is that the nature of the contact of a human with the aumakua depends on the inner consciousness of the human. Like attracts like, and any subjective deception results in an objective distortion. In fulfilling principle number 26, the subdivisions of principle number 24 come into operation. Thus the reason has three aspects: (a) true self-knowledge; (b) authentic initiation, instruction, and application; and (c) discrimination as to what sort of aumakua is contacted.*

Bray goes on to discuss the true structure of the complete person and balancing internal polarity. A Kahuna must master the positive and negative forces. (Not positive and negative as in "right and wrong", but as in electrical polarity.) The positive power works through the heavenly, while the negative works through the material. The material and psychical are sometimes called "earthbound." This means the forces of the negative work through the psychic and earthly elements. The positive is mental, spiritual, and beyond the normal conditions of human life in its physical and emotional aspects.

The polarities must be brought together for completeness and balance. In order to do this, Kahuna have to understand how energy flows through their own bodies. There is a definite localization of positive and negative poles, a pattern for the flow of energy, and a method of harmonization. (See Chart 2 while studying this section of principles.)

31. *All life is a union of positive and negative, but there are two kinds of earthbound, negative forces. The earthbound of the highest represents those forces of nature which work for the harmony of nature, and the benefit of humanity. The lowest force of earthbound works for destruction and selfishness. While learning to distinguish between higher and lower, the Kahuna must learn also to control the lowest earthbound. He cannot turn his back on the lowest earthbound without opening himself to an attack of ignorance, since he cannot escape his own impulses and cannot help those who are sick because of lower influences.*

32. *The way the Kahuna learns about the negative forces of the highest and lowest is through studying every sort of experience. No form of life can be hidden from him, but most of all he must*

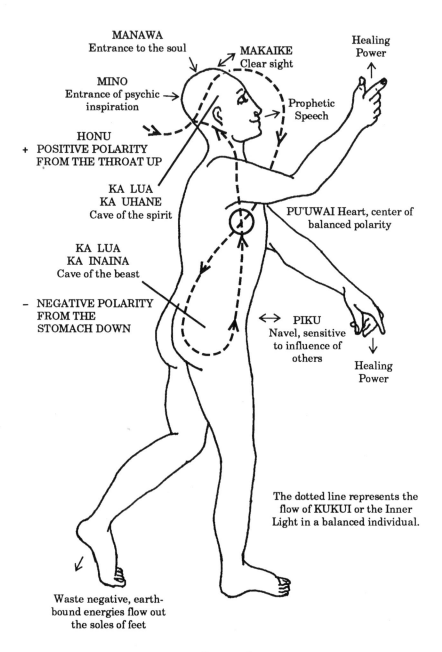

MANAWA
Entrance to the soul

MAKAIKE
Clear sight

Healing
Power

MINO
Entrance of psychic
inspiration

Prophetic
Speech

HONU
+ POSITIVE POLARITY
FROM THE THROAT UP

KA LUA
KA UHANE
Cave of the spirit

PU'UWAI Heart, center of
balanced polarity

KA LUA
KA INAINA
Cave of the beast

− NEGATIVE POLARITY
FROM THE
STOMACH DOWN

PIKU
Navel, sensitive
to influence of
others

Healing
Power

The dotted line represents the
flow of KUKUI or the Inner
Light in a balanced individual.

Waste negative, earth-
bound energies flow out
the soles of feet

CHART 2:
THE HAWAIIAN SYSTEM OF PSYCHIC ENERGY FLOW

learn to know and control the negative forces of his own nature.

33. *Anatomically, the negative polarity is localized from the stomach down through the sex and evacuation organs. This is called Ka Lua Ka Inaina or Cave of the Beast. Besides biological processes, this center is composed mostly of unreal love and attachment to the senses.*

34. *Emotional attachment of unreal love creates negative emotions which attract illusory experiences and the lowest earthbound intelligences. Some of these emotions are: (a) love or craving for the pleasures of this earth; (b) the search for earthly wealth; (c) the search for self-gain and glory; (d) greed; (e) selfishness; (f) envy; (g) lust for things that satisfy the illusion of separation; (h) hate; (i) jealousy; (j) slavery to the will of others; and (k) fear which makes a god of the unreal, which is the strongest of the negative emotions.*

35. *Kahuna do not strive to suppress these emotions, but to understand their sources, how they act, and why they are clung to. The negative is refilled with the positive, but does not vanish. Instead, Kahuna are able to feel negative emotions and release them, thus not being trapped by their consequences. To do this requires meditation and advice from a trained expert.*

36. *"God in us" is discovered by understanding the positive emotions which lead to divine knowledge and attract healthy attitudes and the aumakua of creativity. Some of these virtues are: (a) humbleness, (b) patience, (c) self-control, (d) perseverance, (e) kindness, (f) tolerance, (g) the*

ability to remain undisturbed by obstacles of delay and failure, (h) patience and fairness with those whose opinions and practices differ from one's own, (i) the ability to bear stress and strain, (j) the ability to exercise love and calmness at all times, (k) meditation on the divine nature of the soul, (l) openness to reality, (m) an understanding of the four great elements of life and their interaction to form all processes, and (n) realization of eternal life in the reality of God.

37. *In utilizing number 36, the positive pole is pictured as the area from the throat to a space a few inches above the head. At the base of the skull where the backbone enters is the "Honu" or Entrance for the Mana. Within the head is "Ka Lua Ka Uhane" or the Cave of the Spirit. This cavern is to be filled with the light of the Great Power, and then the light is allowed to circulate through the body.*

38. *When, through the proper use of the steps of meditation described earlier in this chapter, the positive and negative poles are balanced, then the Inner Light or Kukui flows evenly between the Cave of the Spirit and the Cave of the Beast. The Inner Light is renewed constantly by the HONU, which is guarded by the aumakua of the highest kind. The energy flows through the heart as the balancing point. PU'UWAI, or the heart, transforms personal biological, emotional, and mental energies into a universal love energy. The Love Energy manifests in a life of service guided by true spiritual vision, prophetic speech, and healing power.*

39. *The balance of polar forces is always shifting, depending on circumstances and motivation. Too great an emphasis on the intellect and*

*spiritual work can unbalance a person; too great
an emphasis on the pride of accomplishment can
tip the scales to the negative.* The greater the
advancement, the greater the sensitivity to
minor weaknesses.

40. *In all spiritual work, Kahuna become the
negative pole and the aumakua the positive pole.
Because of the internal polar balance, an outer
balance of polarity may be achieved.*

It is important to free the mind and emotions from
outside distractions. We do this through meditation and
prayer. Kahuna do not work for others when filled with
negative emotions or subject to ill health. The mind cannot
be clear under such circumstances, and confusion or illness is projected. Those who deliberately abuse Kahuna
power project this confusion to injure others, but they are
themselves the victims of their methods. When in doubt,
Kahuna rely on the help of their fellow initiates to restore
balance. Kahuna must not only know how to bring balance
in their own lives, but how to counteract the false psychic
power of others and restore balance in the sick and de-
mented. They must be able to remove the hate, envy, and
jealousy of mankind, destroy the evil power of black magic,
and destroy the unreality in mankind. Then there will be
no forces of evil surrounding mankind.

The Kahuna of long ago had much the same ethics as
the better physicians of today. They recognized, however,
that all means of restoring health are really divine healing. The power of life flows from God and gives health, and
its interference or inhibition results in disease.

Kahuna are trained to work with spiritual beings.
Not all aumakua heal. Usually the healing art Kahuna is
inspired by two or three former healers and one or two
high aumakua. These direct him and correct mistakes.
The Kahuna must periodically retire from people and re-
new his contacts and purify himself so that the energy

continues to flow properly. Such retreats are necessary sometimes when dealing with very difficult cases.

41. *Kahuna are the visible links between patients and unseen realities. The patient must consent to treatment, or if unable, a close relative or friend must consent. It is not appropriate to impose the healing art on the unwilling.*

42. *The best information and techniques of physical diagnosis are to be used first.*

43. *Psychologically, the condition of the friends and relatives of the patient should be dealt with, along with the internal problems of the individual (called ho'oponopono).*

44. *Using the "makaike" or true psychic sight, the Kahuna looks directly at the body for dark areas indicating lack of life energy, and abnormally bright areas indicating concentrations of energy due to congestion. The body becomes transparent and the Kahuna pays strict attention to the color and interrelationship of the parts, comparing them with normal health. In doing this, the Kahuna takes note of what activities the patient has been engaged in, for the energy fields of the body shift constantly.*

45. *By making his own body the bridge, the Kahuna contacts his aumakua and directs the proper energy to the proper place and lets the waste drain off through the soles of the feet of the patient.*

46. *Again, using the "makaike," the Kahuna analyzes the thought-forms of the patient which have been created by distorted emotions and thoughts of chronic mental poisoning. These*

may appear as separate beings, but are more similar to the forms which appear in dreams. When habitual, they act as vampires drawing off the life force of the patient. They have no reality in themselves.

47. *To dispel harmful thought-forms, the Kahuna leads the patient to self-awareness by discovering the root of thought-forms, how they function, and why they are clung to. Then the person is free to let go of the thought-form and choose another attitude of mind and emotion, hence a new way of action. The method for doing this can only be gained through experience, since each person is different.*

48. *Sometimes thought-forms are projected upon a person by another. The thought-form must then be exposed as an unreal appearance. If the thought-form has been accepted unconsciously, then the Kahuna must find the weakness in the patient that corresponds to the thought-form. If the thought-form has been accepted consciously, then the Kahuna must discover why the patient does not want to live his own life but conforms to the demands of someone else. In any case, the Kahuna sends the thought-forms back to the sender.*

49. *In a situation where the patient does not have the judgment to differentiate between self and illusion (called false identification), the Kahuna must send the obsessive force back first, then work with the person to bring back the real self.*

50. *Kahuna do not charge for spiritual work. The Great Power and the aumakua work within the patient; the Kahuna works outside. Gifts may be accepted. The Kahuna does not interfere with the*

work of another physician or healer. If the
Kahuna senses disharmony between techniques,
he should not continue the work.

51. *In all healing the Kahuna must always work*
    only up to the level of training and constantly
    realize that all healing is an act of God, not the
    result of personal will.

52. *When possible, healing rituals should be done in*
    cooperation with others who have similar aims
    and training. One person should lead, and the
    others refill that person with light. Leadership
    in ritual healing meditations may rotate through
    the group, and it is helpful for the group to meet
    from time to time on a regular basis.

Although Bray set down these principles, he still
maintained that the details of rituals are best taught
directly after initiation and therefore did not prescribe any
rituals. Rituals were reserved for the initiated.

As we saw in Long's account of the Kahuna tradition,
he emphasizes positive spiritual force and sees healing as
the result of repairing a disruption in the proper order of
things. Bray emphasizes the polarity of spiritual energy
and sees healing resulting from the manipulation of spiritual forces and energy polarities by the Kahuna. The
Kahuna had to be a person of strong physical and spiritual
constitution, someone who could endure the rigors of
preparation for either healing or spiritual exploration and
who could deal with receiving the negative forces by the
person being healed. Bray himself was a physically strong
man, but was often sick from taking on other people's
negativity. Because of his training and commitment he
was willing to do this. It was a conscious choice on his
part. He felt this was his calling and this was his training.
He liked to point to the rainbow, nature's elemental bridge
to the vast multitude of aumakua who served humanity.

"The rainbow commands man to be patient," he would say. "And to keep God's law."

David Bray was a Kahuna who achieved calmness and dignity in character so that the gods trusted him to keep the secrets of nature protected while using wisdom in helping mankind. This is how he is remembered today.

CHAPTER 5

BRIDGES OF CONSCIOUSNESS

*Science now thinks of man's consciousness as a
level of energy.*

We have looked at two versions of the Huna tradition.
However, these are not isolated examples of tribal spiritual traditions throughout the world. We find healers,
shamans, and spiritual leaders in nearly every primitive
society as well as many advanced urban cultures. In this
chapter we will examine some of the shared insights and
understandings common to these traditions. It is interesting that although these traditions evolved separately, they
have a great deal in common. Central to all of these
traditions is the notion that there is some kind of energy
which is the source of action and power.

Max Freedom Long was right when he started from
the point of view that an energy exists which we do not see.
He knew that the Kahuna recognized the nature of this
vital force and that they called it "Mana." To them, it was
the basis of life itself.

Concerning this subtle body energy that surrounds

the body, current researchers report two types of energies: that from normal, healthy bodies, and that from abnormal or diseased bodies. Where disease signals are present, the healthy body signals are generally in a weakened or reduced state. Researchers report that where disease signals (or imbalances) are reduced or eliminated, the healthy body signals generally return to high, or normal levels. The Kahuna eliminated imbalances by projecting high charges of Mana (life force, chi, ki, prana) into a sick person.

Man has proven that by projecting love or positive energy into a plant, it will flourish and grow, just as a child who is injured will run to its mother who will project love (positive energy) to the child, and by doing so will release love or energy and relieve the pain. Brugh Joy, in his classic book on the potentials for healing with body energies, *Joy's Way* (1979), claims that there is no greater gift one can offer than the energy of unconditional love, and that this is the basis for all healing. This love comes from God and is passed on through us.

Long would agree. In 1968 he wrote in "Huna Vistas" that perhaps the answer to instant healing lies some way in our better use of Mana. During such healing, a person becomes a medium for the inflow of the High Self controlled mana. In such a case, the person must possess a great deal of pure love and unselfishness, which is the character of the Higher Self (Christ Consciousness- the Father in Heaven within). This is no doubt what achieves instant healing and even slower healing in small degrees.

David Bray also understood and worked with energies. Being particularly interested and oriented toward the chakra system, he organized energy in these terms.

The chakras are organs of psychic perception. There are seven main chakras. [See Chart 3.]

Crown: *The highest subtle center of consciousness, the crown chakra, the thousand-*

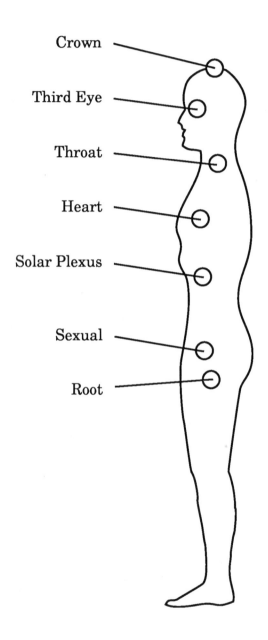

Crown

Third Eye

Throat

Heart

Solar Plexus

Sexual

Root

CHART 3: THE CHAKRA SYSTEM

petaled lotus, that which unites man with the infinite.

Third Eye: *Situated between the eyebrows, it is sometimes called the third eye. This center forms the organ of psychic visualization or clairvoyance.*

Throat: *Situated at the throat, this chakra mediates vocal expression.*

Heart: *Situated in the cardiac region, this chakra mediates the emotions of love and devotion.*

Solar Plexus: *Located at the level of the solar plexus, this is the power chakra and mediates one's ability to control situations.*

Sexual: *This chakra is situated in the genital area and is associated with the exchange of sexual energies.*

Root: *Situated at the base of the spinal column between the anus and the genitals, this center is the seat of a psychic form of energy known as kundalini; it also mediates the survival needs of the organism.*

Bray believed that the lower three chakras are used to bring the Mana or universal energy into the physical body so that one can use it and direct it at will. It is the fourth, or Heart Chakra, that is used to TRANSFORM the energies into a higher frequency of unconditional love for one's fellow man.

The heart chakra is where you begin to combine with your fellow man by bringing into your own consciousness a realization that you are not alone.

The heart is also a place where you change from being a crusader into being a warrior. We in Hawaii used to say,

"It is when the man becomes God." In other words, when you combine that which you desire for yourself with an understanding and awareness of what is best for those around you, that is changing into a God. Crusaders try to change the world. *Warriors change themselves, and by doing so, effect a change in the world.*

At the fifth or throat chakra you begin to connect up to the higher frequencies of your own intuitive awareness.

The accuracy and power of your psychic abilities depend upon how much energy is flowing in a balanced manner through your own chakra system. Your Aumakua (high self, god-self, super conscious mind), your own spirit guides who assist you in your present spiritual path, work through the intuition centers in your soul-conscious, seventh chakra and your third eye, sixth chakra. They are able to vibrate at the same kind of frequency as the energy of these two chakras. They can unite with your mind and continue to bring you information as you need it.

The fourth chakra energy of unconditional love which both Long and Bray, as well as many others, recognized, is the bridge which takes one from the conscious to the unconscious. Energy is the motivating factor in making the bridge. The energy of unconditional love enables us to dig into our unconscious and examine destructive and negative programming which is keeping us from making contact with our Higher Self. Once we establish contact with our Higher Self we are able to direct this energy of unconditional love at will.

Unconditional love is the force; the wisdom we gain through our experiences is the discretion behind the force. We need the wisdom to appreciate the force. We need to learn discretion, the first step along the path. For example, if someone were thirsty and we were standing there with a heavy duty fire hose used in fighting fires, what would happen if we turned and pointed it in the direction of his mouth? We would knock him over and perhaps injure him as a result of using so much force. So it is with directing the force of unconditional love at people. Picture someone's heart chakra. Now visualize sending him unconditional love going in through his heart chakra. In order to do this, we need to be in touch with how open his chakra is, for he can only absorb the amount to which he is open. The rest will run off and if sent with too much force will knock him over in the process. If this happens, we need to learn how to step back and lovingly dissociate ourselves from him until he is able to pick himself up again. Bowling people over and blowing them away does nothing more than feed our own egos, something we still desire to do because we have not yet become balanced.

The heart, as the bridge of unconditional love that transmutes unwanted thought patterns and energies, makes the conscious and unconscious one. It is the vehicle by which we pass over from negative to positive, fear to courage, hate to love, death to rebirth, despair to hope, living in the past or future to living in the present magical moment of now.

It is what all of us want and it can be ours if we will take the time to listen to the still small voice and have the discipline to be willing to do whatever it takes. The still small voice never goes against our heart's desire. It is so important to remember this. We will, however, be tested as to our willingness to move from our position even though we may not actually have to do so.

Unconditional love is the force that balances us. Tune into the voice. It brings peace, harmony and love to our lives.

The bridge is the heart, the destroyer of the ego. It is the ego that separates the conscious and unconscious. The ego is an accumulation of ways to get attention and acts as a barrier between the conscious and unconscious mind. It keeps us from pure awareness, which is our true identity. The ego is an accumulation of our outer world experiences, and these experiences create an "I." Ego is in separation from the "I AM" presence of God, so it is a crowd, a bunch of diverse things we have paid attention to, rather than a constant self-maintaining. *Ego is another word for fear.* Pride is the power of the ego to defend itself and its position. "To destroy the ego and come off our position is to rediscover ourself and merge with Spirit. By doing this we gain freedom, which is the ability to stand clear in God self.

By merging with God we rediscover our soul. Much has been written and speculated about the soul. The soul is our inner light, our link with God. Paul Brunton, in *The Secret Path* (1935, p. 35), says,

> *God has sent a true light into the heart of every child that is born, but it must be unveiled. This true light is the soul, and it is never lost. Saints, sages, thinkers and philosophers, priest and scientific inquirers have tried for centuries to understand the nature of the human soul. It is a paradoxical being— capable of descent into evil and soaring nobility.*

Edward Bach (1977) said, to remember that for each person his soul has laid down a particular work for him, and that unless he does his work, though perhaps not consciously, he will find a conflict between his Soul and personality which of necessity will react in the form of a physical disorder.

But all that one is asked to give up in the name of spiritual development, which is the path of the soul's highest development, will be given back tenfold, sometimes in ways which are at first unrecognizable. We give up our ego, so that we may gain unity with our soul. At first we are unwilling and afraid to give up the comfort of our ego, but as we gain more and more contact with our soul through our inner knowledge of God, we become more comfortable in letting go of our attachments to the outer trappings.

Our Aumakua (high self, god-self, super conscious mind) is the highest within us, it is the oneness of God expressed through us, an expression of light. Power is our ability to surrender to the highest within and channel it so to reflect it back out into the world.

Everyone who is able to go in and out of the conscious and unconscious worlds are able to do so at will in accordance with the degree to which they are willing to acknowledge God in their life, for God is the bridge between the two worlds.

"Ask and it will be given to you. Search and you will find. Knock and the door will be opened for you. The one who asks will always receive; the one who is searching will always find, and the door is opened to the man who knocks." (Matthew 7:7)

"Seek ye first the kingdom of Heaven within." (Matthew 6:33)

Paramahansa Yogananda, the founder of the Self-Realization Fellowship in America said,

"I am infinite. I am spaceless, I am tireless; I am beyond body, thought, and utterance; beyond all matter and mind. I am endless bliss. I am submerged in Thine eternal Light; it permeates every particle of my being; I am living in that Light, Divine Spirit, I behold only Thee, Within and Without." (1969)

To serve mankind as one's larger Self is the goal. Spirit is one. The purpose in life is to reflect this oneness. Freedom is won individually from within, not from any teachings or teacher, and this is why early Kahuna training to trust in oneself is so important. Aligning to these goals brings clarity.

Meditation is a way to merge with Spirit. It gives us a depth of being within to take to the outer world. Meditation takes us to the state of pure awareness which is our true identity. Meditation is a movement of consciousness. Meditation is a tool we can use to go within, discover Spirit, and in the process lose our ego and fear and find love, our true nature.

Let's look at the subtle differences between the levels of vibration that take us to Spirit. Merging with Spirit, the total destruction of the ego and meshing of the conscious and unconscious states, is a state indescribable in words. It is a mystic state, capable of being experienced and talked about, but never fully and completely captured by words because the element of experience is always elusive of words.

Modern linguists tell us that language can only describe an experience, never become the experience itself. But before the development of civilization, humans had no compulsion to talk about their experiences; they merely experienced them. Early man followed his hunches and developed his intuition. Mystical states were commonplace for him.

As man gradually began to move to cities, he began to analyze these experiences. In the process, he began to doubt the validity of the experiences themselves, putting trust more and more in the spoken word and the ability to convince one's neighbor or friend of the reality of the experience.

This also resulted in the time distortion we now experience, and the lack of ability to experience the moment. Often, rather than experiencing the moment, we are thinking about it in terms of language and sometimes even going so far as to think, "Wait until I tell so-and-so what happened." The moment is lost through language in a sense. Because of this, meditation plays an important part in taking us back to the experience in its pure form because it eliminates analysis.

In meditation, when the mind becomes silent and we become more finely aware, things which were below our conscious awareness become observable to us, and through our awareness of these things we begin to integrate them into our conscious mind. This is the process of meditation. Going within and dredging up past memories and events. Learning to love ourselves, which we do through God's love for us. In the process we need to learn to be patient with ourselves.

As we focus our attention in meditation the levels of consciousness we pass through become more and more subtle then we merge with God.

Knowledge we gain in meditation gives us freedom, which is power, bringing with it a responsibility. This is why true spiritual power is never given to one with a large ego. The very process of attaining spiritual power is the process of *losing* the ego. Spiritual freedom is to be without an ego and to be free to merge with God at will.

A mystic unfolds the mysteries by experiencing the levels of consciousness. A fully conscious being cannot be controlled. To be fully conscious means you are experiencing ALL levels of consciousness. To experience God-consciousness you obtain the stillness within, which is your light being qualified.

The great seers were *see-ers*, not lookers. In order to do so, they put their ego and personality aside and were able to stand free and clear and unattached. The "light workers" of this planet are those who are standing in the I AM presence.

The Ancient Hawaiians had a chant describing this, called *Ho'opuka E-Ka-La Ma Kahikina*, to "invoke the dawning of enlightenment". It is reproduced here from the forth coming book by Tad James and George Naope (1991).

Ho'opuka e-ka-la ma ka hikina

Me kahua ka'i hele no tumutahi

Ha'a mai nai wa me Hi'iaka

Me Tapo Laka ika ulu wehiwehi

Ne'e mai nai wa ma ku'u alo

Ho'i no e te tapu me Na'ali'i e...

E ola makou a mau loa lae

He inoa no ma ka hikina

In English, as translated by James (1989)

"Make a hole in the sunlight and find the light behind the light. Like the sunrise come and dawn on me.

From your foundation, lift up; Move from your origin.

By means of breath come to me. Take me by force loudly as Hi'iaka, Goddess of healing.

Revolve, take me, drift upon me, increase, spread, as I hear this song, the means of life from God.

Creeping along like the lava, come to me! Take me by force loudly.

By means of release, come and be with me.

Cause meditation to come to me by means of this sacred ceremony belonging to the ali'i (royalty).

By means of the spiritual food, we acquire the means of life forever, and permanent wisdom.

A chant in the honor of the Dawning of Enlightenment.

In our exploration of the levels of consciousness we can call on the hierarchy of light to assist us. The hierarchy of light begins with the elementals:

1. ***Earth:*** *solid, grounding (represented by Pele, and called Honua in Hawaiian).*

2. **Water:** *fluid, cooling, fills things up (represented by Manu, Wai in Hawaiian).*

3. **Air:** *breath, sky, free to go and loves to blow (represented by Pueo and called Ha in Hawaiian).*

4. **Fire:** *light, heat, catalyst, a rebel (represented by Mo'o, and called Ahi in Hawaiian).*

5. **Ether:** *spirit, void, lightness (called I'o in Hawaiian).*

After the elementals come the *Ascending Masters.* They are the masters who are on the planet now, such a Sai Baba and the Dalai Lama. Next, the *Ascended Masters* are those who made it through and are there to back you up and add the power of overcoming. Next, the *Angels* are those beings supporting manifestation. They are there for you to call on for help and seek expression through you. Next, the *Archangels,* who form the *arch* from God to man.

Above the Archangels come the cosmic beings, Cosmic Christ, the Great and Holy Spirit, the I AM presence, and then the One Without a Second, God.

In exploring the levels of consciousness on a spiritual path, the principles of expression are: The Light never fails. Knock and the door shall open. Seek and ye shall find. Ask and it shall be given. The call compels the answer.

The Aumakua (high self, god-self, super conscious mind), which is the highest within you, is the oneness of God expressed through you. You are an expression of light. Your power is the ability to surrender to the highest within you and channel it in order to reflect it back out into the world. We go within to express outwardly.

Salvation is the salvaging of the *attention* you give away on negative and unwanted thoughts. Your freedom is the ability to stand clear in God self. The master has the controlled ability to impress with light. This is his power.

He is able to harness energy. *The choices you make qualify the light within you as it reflects back outward.*

The power of mastery in consciousness takes place on nine levels: physical, emotional, thinking mind, knowledge, creative, imagination, universal mind, mastery, and Christ mind. In your search, remember that the enlightened beings who have seen the truth will instruct you in knowledge. There is a cosmic law that states, "The call compels the answer." This is a cosmic law of the universe and thus above parental law and natural law. The path to God is reverent submission and earnest inquiry. *The same Light comes to you as comes to all. It is filtered through your qualifications.*

Do whatever it takes. Knowledge is freedom. Freedom is power. Power brings responsibility. You are the Creator localized. Fill your life with purpose and direction and perfect the diamond clarity of your being. Remember that the promise of the universe is unconditional love; and that this promises the forgiveness for all mistakes made in the search for truth.

By examining several spiritual traditions, we have seen how the inner voice is the heart and the other outer voices are the ego. By tuning into the inner voice of the heart, we create balance through love and destroy the ego. By destroying the ego we merge with God, thereby gaining freedom of the soul. One of the ways to do this is through meditation. Now let us take another look at the teachings of Long and Bray in the light of all this and see what conclusions we can draw.

CHAPTER 6

HOW THE KAHUNA HEAL

*We are able to create our future the way we want it.
The same is true of the past and the present.*

Max Freedom Long and David Kaonohiokala Bray were both men who devoted their lives to the spreading of the Huna tradition. Both were interested in healing. It is interesting to note that Bray started within the Hawaiian tradition and reached out to teach the Western world, while Long started within the Western tradition and reached out into the Hawaiian culture. Both were pioneers. Both wanted to better the world. Both were interested in healing and sought out its mysteries.

Bray was able to *perform the acts of healing* that Long strove to understand by creating an elaborate system of Huna psychology in order to explain the phenomena. In so doing, Long became a moving force in the healing of the rift that had developed within the Hawaiians themselves between their ancient beliefs and the new world into which they were thrust once the missionaries stepped foot on their Islands and brought with them changes in their belief system. In this sense, *Bray and Long were both healers,* each doing what he knew how to within the framework of his individual belief system.

My belief is that what Long discovered in the code was correct and yet was not *all* of Kahuna knowledge. As both Long and Bray would agree, the Kahuna were very elusive. Long found it to be so in his search for answers, while Bray says that a Kahuna never tells 100%, but that he tells only about 80%.

Kahuna knowledge is only passed on from the master when the student can demonstrate what is to be taught. The student has to learn it on his own, by using his integrated knowledge, and once he has learned it he demonstrates it to his Kahuna teacher, who then confirms what he has just taught himself. Then, like in the Zen tradition, the Kahuna points the student in the next appropriate direction. This is one way the secrets are kept carefully guarded from any who would use them in any way other than to serve humanity.

The Kahuna never coded their system of knowledge in any way that could be decoded by someone who did not have the proper training and preparation. Bray says of Long, "he opened the door for the way of Kahunaism to the world but he did not have all the answers." This is probably so, but I believe even Bray knew more than he was willing to let on. He said as much himself. In addition to this, *his knowledge and understanding were evolving and growing even during his lifetime.* Similarly, the Kahuna system of knowledge is not a closed system, but rather a changing and evolving one which depends upon the new Kahuna who are born into each new generation to leave their mark upon the tradition.

This is one reason why it is so important to establish contact with one's Aumakua (high self, god-self, super conscious mind), and aumakua (a general term for spirits and or gods, usually helpful), and listen to whatever it is they have to say. They are only interested in the betterment of the world, and by listening to them and following their guidance we can insure a proper future for the world we love.

Bray says that Long's system is a closed system because he has the Low Self talking to the High Self, which creates a separation between the two parts. (In Bray's system, the division into 3 selves was simply a metaphor.) Bray also believed in establishing contact with higher powers outside oneself. This expanded system includes the possibility of powers higher than oneself. This system is open for each generation to add their own experience—a truly open system indeed!

Kahuna are brought up to learn through experience. Each experience is different because it is viewed through the filters of past experiences. Thus, each generation of Kahuna experiences the world differently because the world, as well as themselves, is changing. *The body of knowledge is constantly evolving and changing.*

A lot has been written lamenting the fact that so much knowledge from the past has been lost forever, that all the Kahuna who knew the most carefully guarded secrets of old are now dead, and nothing can be done in this day and age to rescue the lost past. My feeling is that we may not have all the specific knowledge from their past, but *we do have what is appropriate and necessary to our present.* In other words, we have what we need from the past. Bray told Charlton not to go to the past for all the information and answers because the vibration has already changed. (Charlton, Eileen, 1981)

Charlton said, that which has passed out of physical existence has passed. The vibration of the planet earth continues to evolve. You can learn from the past, you can understand yourself by understanding the past, but to try to recreate something that has gone on before you is a waste of time. Look to the future and to the present, not the past.

Every single decision you make shapes your future.

There are high, *high* aumakua helping to balance, helping to create, helping to keep the planet stable. But the plan is not set—it is created anew every day through choice, through free will, through emotions, through desires, and through spiritual laws. Your energy, combined with those of mankind, creates your world.

It is important to look to yourself and to the future. There are many people who are now "passed on" who are waiting for us to seek them out and ask for their interpretation of what they felt and believed during their life on earth in light of their present broader perspective of having "passed on". It is a group effort on the part of everyone who has walked this earth to guide it to its logical path of evolution, whatever that may be. Buckminster Fuller expresses this point of view in his book Critical Path (1981), when he says that effective decisions can only be made by independently thinking and adequately informed human individuals and their telepathically intercommunicated wisdom.

The answers lie within each of us. When we see that within us all is God, the spark of the divine, when we set our own course and follow it, we will lose our dissatisfaction, anger, despair, and work together with our fellow man toward the well-being of all humanity.

Long and Bray were both men who felt this way. They were interested in the evolution of mankind and worked toward its betterment. That they did so within different frameworks is of no real consequence in the long run. That they *did* so is what matters. They were both men of vision of a hope for a better future. They were working toward the same goal.

The writing of this book has been a personal journey in experiencing the levels of consciousness and making the bridge between the conscious and unconscious. Doing so was an act of faith which led eventually to understanding.

In order to do so, I was guided to go to the island of Kaua'i in the Hawaiian Islands. Just before I left for the island, the book *Past Lives, Future Loves* (1978) by Dick Sutphen was given to me. The book fell open and I read about an Indian legend about the four places in the world designated as "power spots"—two positive and two negative or two "light" and two "dark." It is believed that the two "positive" places in the world are Hawaii, and Sedona. Both are red-rock countries. Sedona and Kaua'i, the Indians say, are vortexes of energy in which the Great Spirit gives birth to rainbows.

As I began to contact Puna, my own personal Aumakua, more and more, I began to develop a great respect for her and came to realize her place in my life as my own personal Aumakua. She was there to protect me and answer certain questions when I contacted her in meditation. I had gone to Kaua'i basically because I had felt called there, but what I was looking for could only be found within me. I could not deny this any longer, Puna was a part of me, as much as my living and breathing daughter was. I needed to find a way to establish better and better communication between the two of us, and since I knew she was always there waiting for me, I realized this would have to come from me.

As I turned inward, it began as kind of a lark to interview Puna, but it grew into a relationship that changed and expanded. I was very skeptical at first. However, as I went along, it became more and more natural and besides, it was what I was experiencing.

One of the first things Puna told me was that every age had its own particular wisdom and something to contribute to the ongoing saga of history. I would always be learning and growing. Everyone has to initiate themselves because the knowledge is within. I began to go deeper within myself, doing what was required of me for my spiritual growth.

Prayer has begun to hold a particular interest for me. Its importance in all types of healing, spiritual, physical, emotional, and mental, became increasingly clear to me.

Prayer is what gives healing its potency and power. It is in the act of praying that one establishes oneself as pure in mind and spirit and therefore able to contact whoever it is one is praying to in order to get results. Prayer is the essence of a person's beliefs. *Those who **know how** to pray have their prayers answered.*

The Hawaiian Kahuna chanted their prayers and knew that prayer is the uniting factor between the separate selves. Long says that in prayer the low self contacts the High Self. Bray feels that in prayer the selves of man must first be united and balanced and then reach out beyond the limited self to a greater power. Whichever way you look at it, the selves must be united and balanced in order to achieve effective prayer. If the prayer is from the emotional level of the individual it will have great personal meaning and effect.

Prayer is an experience. No one can teach you about prayer beyond the mechanics and theory. After that you are on your own to find something about which you care deeply and find a way in your heart to make contact with God. The contact is very important. Just saying the words is not praying.

Once on Kaua'i when things seemed their bleakest and I felt as though I could not go on, I got down on my knees with tears streaming down my face. "Dear God," I prayed, "I believe I am in the right place, doing what You want me to be doing. If this is so, You have got to send me someone, for I need someone." I prayed this with all my heart. All of a sudden a very warm peaceful feeling came over me and I knew things would be okay. I was "told" where to go the next day, and when I did so, I met the someone for whom I had prayed.

A great American Indian medicine man, Lame Deer, says (1972), that when an Indian prays he doesn't just read words out of a book. He says a very short prayer. If you say a long one your Unihipili (lower self, unconscious mind, body-mind) won't understand what you are saying.

The Indian medicine man is one who is in touch with his low self. He IS the earth, the fire, the winds, the water. Everything in nature he sees as an extension of himself. He imagines his feet grow down into the Earth, as the roots of a tree; and in this manner he is one with the earth. Indeed, his powers come from the elements of nature. He is in effortless contact with his low self and finds it very easy to offer this simple prayer, directly to the Great Spirit, full of emotion and mana. *Because he is balanced, the forces of nature trust him and reveal their secrets to him.*

Through all of my research and reading I kept looking for an answer to the question, "How do the Kahuna heal?" It is the same question to which Long devoted his life and the question that Bray attempted to answer by sharing his experiences with non-Hawaiians. In all my searching I kept getting the answer over and over again: "Go within. The answers are all within." All the great teachers down through the ages taught this message.

Healing is a vast subject and the question of how a Kahuna heals is a difficult one indeed. A metaphysical healer acts today as if someone, or anyone, is going to call tomorrow and ask for help. They treat everyone in this way, as a potential client. They have no emotions of hate, fear, or judgments. One cannot heal when one is holding someone in condemnation of his offenses. There is no spiritual love in condemnation.

There is spiritual love in forgiveness. Spiritual power, or "ike," is something that comes to us when our thought has stopped and we no longer have thoughts, wishes, or desires. It is then that we are able to sit and inwardly listen and wait for inward illumination from God. All things can be done through God.

Spiritual healing work dissolves the material sense. It is the belief in the cause of illness that creates the illness. When there is no personal sense of "I" left, we have only God. God realization is the dissolving of the ego. Our own inner realization of God is what does the work of healing. We attract to us only an inner realization of God's presence and His unfolding does the rest. Higher consciousness is the consciousness of God and His power. Pure consciousness in the higher state is creativeness of all that is. God is one. God is one power.

Healing is just revealing the presence of God in your life. The word HEAL can be separated to HE-AL. When you experience HE (God) as AL, you experience healing. Standing in the presence is standing in the light and heals.

There is a difference in cognitive and intuitive teaching. The attitude for spiritual teaching is that the teacher at that moment is the master and the student at that moment is the student. This is the relationship that must be established with one's Aumakua. No student who is ever a student can believe that he knows enough to discuss truth with his Kahuna teacher. No Kahuna teacher will believe that truth will be learned through discussion, conversation, or the question and answer method. That is why spiritual teaching is done in parables, metaphors and by experience. No one can tell you the truth, only lead you to it of your own accord.

Long and Bray addressed themselves to the same question, "How do the Kahuna heal?" They approached it from different points of view. Neither was right or wrong. Neither had all the answers. Long was able to discuss and project theories as to how the Kahuna heal. Bray was able to heal and discuss certain aspects of how he healed; however, he reserved the right not to pass on certain information to other than a chosen few. Long felt the information he discovered was to be made available to anyone who was interested and carried out scientific investigation. Both Bray and Long went within and discovered their own inner truths. *Each did what they did because they felt guided to do so and it was the truth for them.*

We each have separate information and yet because we are part of the One it is all available to each of us if we but open ourselves to it. There are no gurus outside ourselves. Not only do we have to figure out all the answers for ourselves; *we have to figure out the questions as well.*

The Hawaiian Kahuna are able to heal because they have gone within, figured out the questions to ask and then answered them. They have meditated on the meaning of things and explored their deepest nature. In so doing they have come to understand themselves. In understanding themselves they have understood their connectedness with everything else in nature, for everything operates under the same laws. Truth is understood and recognized by all who seek it.

By understanding nature they have won the respect and trust of natural forces and are able to work with them. By working with them according to these laws, they are able to perform extraordinary feats not understood by many. All these abilities are available to those who are willing to pursue the path that leads to their understanding and unfoldment. The path is narrow and discrimination and perseverance are required.

The universe supports us. With purpose and direction the universe knows where we want to go and sends us there. However, purpose and direction grow out of confusion and paradoxes, so we must be open to new direction and purposes. The way to do this is to surrender to God's purpose and direction in our lives by *turning inward and listening* to the voice within.

We do not truly grow until there is mutual acceptance through commitment in a relationship which needs to be expanded to humanity as a whole. We are all searching for the same thing and headed toward the same direction. We are all mirrors for one another.

Wherever we go, there we are.

When we turn inward to reach that deep core within us, we can't help but take it back out into the world with us. We change the world by changing ourselves.

CHAPTER 7

THE JOURNEY CONCLUDES

Balance, and the ability to re-establish balance at will is the key.

The key to becoming a strong, self-contained Kahuna means creating an inner balance so strong that nothing in the external material world or the internal spiritual world can throw one off center without the individual being aware of it and possessing the ability to *re-establish that balance at will.* The reason for this is that balance is not a static state that, once achieved, remains forever. Balance is ever changing, constantly shifting and rearranging itself in order to be established. There is no such thing as static balance. Therefore, in order to experience balance, a Kahuna must learn to constantly shift and rearrange himself or herself according to the exterior world he or she is experiencing. And experience is the key.

Just as the balance within the Kahuna is shifting, so is the balance between the physical and spiritual worlds in which the Kahuna lives. Just as the Kahuna is evolving in this lifetime, so are his Aumakua, in the spirit world. In order to pass on information, the Aumakua must also evolve along with the world, or their information will be outdated and irrelevant. The Kahuna must remember this and maintain the proper balance. While maintaining an inner balance and respect for his Aumakua, the Kahuna must at the same time establish himself or herself as the one with free will. He or she is, after all, the one inhabiting the body, and has some rights to what it is used for and when. The communication between Aumakua and Kahuna must be kept open and an inner dialogue pursued at all times. Each must be kept happy and do his or her share.

The study of higher consciousness is the study and development of that part of the mind we don't ordinarily use. We need to learn new ways of thinking in order not to be frustrated in our thinking and problem solving. Getting to know and communicating with your own Aumakua is a new way of thinking that can open your mind and experiences to a new state of consciousness and help you know the truth about how the mind works. Then you will be able to use these truths to create the things you want, to be aware of what you want, and to *create consciously.*

The writing of this book has been much like putting together the pieces of a jigsaw puzzle. It is the story of a process, not a static event. It is the interaction of writer and reader; the effect one has upon the other. In my writing I have wanted to give the reader the freedom to interact with the printed word at whatever level is appropriate.

I remember when I had my daughter, the actual birth was very easy. I discovered, however, that although I had done the work of producing the baby, the work of loving and raising it had just begun.

In putting together this book, I have often felt I was giving birth. I suppose every author feels this way. The birthing of a new idea is intense and painful at times. It means the giving up of old ways and the leaving behind of some things. I have also found that my work is not over now that I have completed the writing. The writing may be over, but now it is time for us to go out and live these principles.

Life is to be lived. Thank you for reading along with me. May the paths we take along life's journey intersect along the way. I love you.

Me ke aloha pumehana.

GLOSSARY

Aina — land.

Aka — lit. etheric substance, which is sticky, and provides a medium for the transmission of information and energy.

Aloha — lit. my life's breath (ha) goes with you (alo).

Ana'ana — sorcery. lit. a death prayer.

aumakua — (not capitalized) a grab-bag term for any spirit of a higher level than the human being including angels, and gods.

Aumakua — (capitalized) the higher self, superconscious mind, god-self.

Aura — energy field which surrounds the human body.

Body-mind — the mind of the body, or the part of the mind that runs the body.

Chakra — one of the seven energy centers contained in one of the non-physical bodies.

Chi — a Chinese word for life's force, or energy.

Cleansing — in Hawaiian, 'kala', clearing unwanted negative energies from the aura.

Clearing — removing complexes, fixations, guilt and false identifications.

Counter-sorcery — means taken to avoid the effects of sorcery.

Etheric Substance — non-physical substance which is sticky, and provides a medium for the transmission of information and energy.

Fixation — fetish, infatuation, obsession, passion, or preoccupation.

God-self — higher self, or Aumakua.

Gurdjieff — one of the primary, seminal metaphysical teachers in the western world who lived in England in the early 20th century.

Ha — lit. breath, also life's breath, four.

Haole — lit. without (ole) breath (ha). The Hawaiians observed that when the missionaries prayed that they did so without taking a breath first, and so called them haole.

Healing — any physical or mental therapeutic process.

Hi'iaka — ancient Hawaiian goddess of healing.

High Self — superconscious mind, or god-self.

Honu — a hole for higher Mana or light to flow into the body.

Honua — earth.

Ho'oponopono — lit. to make (ho'o) right (pono). The process involved making amends with the family (ohana) and the departed ancestors.

Huna — lit. secret, any teaching that was not immediately obvious, and which may take a little more time to learn.

Hypnosis — the process of inducing trance in yourself or another.

I'o — lit. truth, the great unmanifest, akasha.

Ihowa — God.

Ike — supreme vision, the ability to see non-material things.

Inoa — lit. name.

Invocation — to invoke a spirit or god.

Kahu — lit. keeper, or priest who keeps the knowledge.

Kahuna — lit. keeper (kahu) of something (na) which is secret (huna).

Kahunaism — the teaching of a Kahuna.

Kala — lit. the (ka) light (la), also cleansing.

Kalani — the heavens.

Kalakaua — King of Hawaii who reigned from 1874 to 1891, called the merry monarch, he was responsible for the revival of the hula around 1875.

Kamehameha — King of Hawaii. Kamehameha I was born in 1736, he united the Hawaiian islands by conquest in approx. 1810, he reigned until his death in 1819.

Kanaloa — one of the four major gods of ancient Hawaii.

Kane — one of the four major gods of ancient Hawaii. If not capitalized, another name for the higher self.

Kaonohiokala — lit. the seeing eye of the sun, David Bray, Sr.'s Hawaiian name.

Kapu — tapu, taboo, restriction, prohibition, or constraint.

Kaua'i — one of the major islands in Hawaii.

Ke — lit. the.

Kealoha — lit. the (ke) love (aloha).

Keiki — lit. child.

Ki — a Japanese word for life's force, or energy. The Hawaiian word is mana.

Ki'i — lit. image.

Kino-aka — one of the bodies (kino) of etheric substance (aka).

Ku — one of the four major gods of ancient Hawaii. If not capitalized, the unconscious mind.

Kumu — lit. teacher.

Kundalini — the spiritual energy force that manifests in the body in the spine. In eastern teaching, it lies dormant at the base of the spine.

Kupuna — lit. grandparents.

La'au lapa'au — medical doctor.

Laka — in ancient Hawaii, the goddess of light and of the hula.

Loa — lit. highest.

Lono — one of the four major gods of ancient Hawaii.

Makou — lit. us.

Mana — lit. power. Also the animating energy that runs the body, prana, shakti, life's force.

Mana-loa — the highest (loa) mana, or energy that flows down from the higher self and above.

Mana-mana — the mana that is used by the conscious mind for the process of thinking and its other functions.

Mana-o — lit. the mind.

Manu — lit. bird.

Mesmerism — a process of healing using energy transmission invented by Franz Anton Mesmer in the 17th century.

Middle Self — the conscious mind, also Uhane.

Na — lit. something.

Na'au — lit. guts, located in the area of the navel.

Ohana — lit. family.

Orgone — another word for life's force, chi, ki, shakti or mana used by Wilhelm Reich in the 1950's.

Ouspensky — one of the primary, seminal metaphysical teachers in the western world who lived in England in the early 20th century.

Oukou — lit. your (plural).

Paracelsus — a doctor (who lived from 1490 to 1541) who healed people using magnets.

Patanjali — an early (he lived sometime between 400 BC to 400 AD) creator of yoga.

Poe Aumakua — the collection of all Aumakua.

Po'o — lit. head.

Prana — energy, life's force.

PSI — psychic phenomena.

Tapu — kapu, taboo, restriction, prohibition, or constraint.

Uhane — lit. spirit, conscious mind.

Unihipili — a term used to indicate a spirit that was on a level equivalent to or below the unconscious mind.

BIBLIOGRAPHY

Bach, Edward. 1977. *The Bach Flower Remedies.* New Canaan, Connecticut: Keats Publishing, Inc.

Bach, Richard. 1970. *Jonathan Livingston Seagull.* New York: The Macmillan Company.

Boone, Reverend William F. 1977. *The Secret Gospel Light and Works of Huna.* Nos. 1-8. San Diego, California: Huna Fellowship

Boyd, Doug. 1974. *Rolling Thunder.* New York: Dell Publishing Co., Inc.

Bray, David K. 1963a. "Kahuna Religion of Hawaii." #63403, Tapes 1 and 2. Talking at Galveston, Texas, April 3. Distributed by Borderline Sciences Research Foundation, Vista, California, 1980.

Bray, David K. 1963b. "Kahuna Religion of Hawaii." #630221-A, Tapes 1, 2, and 3. Speaking at Los Angeles. Distributed by Borderline Sciences Research Foundation, Vista, California, 1980.

Bray, David K. 1964. "Kahuna Religion of Hawaii." #64601, Tape. Speaking at Honolulu, June 1. Distributed by Borderline Sciences Research Foundation, Vista, California, 1980.

Bray, David K., and Douglas Low. 1980. *The Kahuna Religion of Hawaii,* ed. Riley Hansard Crabb. Vista, California: Borline Sciences Research Foundation.

Brenner, Paul. 1981. *Life is a Shared Creation.* Marina del Rey, California: DeVorss and Company, Publishers.

Brunton, Paul. 1935. *The Secret Path.* New York: E. P. Dutton.

Cady, Peter. 1981 Taped conversation, Kauai, Hawaii, April 25.

Charlton, Eileen. 1981. Lessons from my Kahuna-teacher. *Huna Vistas,* June, pp. 6-12.

Computer Search, University of California at San Diego Library, for "Kahuna." 1980. Done by Bibliographic Retrieval services, Inc., Scotia, New York.

Deer, John Fire Lame, and Richard Erdoes. 1972. *Lame Deer Seeker of Visions.* New York: Simon and Schuster.

Daws, Gavan. *Shoal of Time: A History of the Hawaiian Islands.*

Honolulu, Hawaii: The University Press of Hawaii, 1968.
Ellis, William. *Polynesian Researches: Hawaii*. Tokyo: Charles E. Tuttle Co., 1969.
Fornander, Abraham. *An Account of the Polynesian Race*. Tokyo: Charles E. Tuttle Co., 1969.
French, Ann Schilt. *Stories of Hawaii*. Boston: Houghton Mifflin Co., 1933.
Fuller, Buckminster. 1981. *Critical Path*. New York: St. Martin's Press.
Gawain, Shakti. *Creative Visualization*. Berkeley, California: Whatever Publishing, 1978.
Glover, William R. 1979. *Huna, The Ancient Religion of Positive Thinking*. Cape Girardeau, Missouri: Huna Press.
Goldstein, Joseph. 1967. *The Experience of Insight: A Natural Unfolding*. Santa Cruz, California: Unity Press.
Gutmanis, June. 1977. *Kahuna La'au Lapa'au*. Norfork Island, Australia: Island Heritage Limited.
Hall, Manley Palmer. *The Secret Teachings of All Ages*. Los Angeles: Philosophical Research Society, 1973.
Hoffman, Enid. 1973. *Huna: A Beginner's Guide*. Rockport, Massachusetts: Para Research, Inc.
Hulme Kathryn. 1966. *Undiscovered Country: In Search of Gurdjieff*. Boston: Little, Brown and Company.
James, W. *The Varieties of Religious Experience*. New York: Longmans, Green, 1902.
Jampolsky, Gerald G. 1979. *Love is Letting Go of Fear*. Millbrae, California: Celestial Arts.
Joy, W. Brugh. 1979. *Joy's Way*. Los Angeles: J. P. Tarcher, Inc.
Judd, Gerrit P., IV. *Hawaii: An Informal History*. New York: Collier Books, 1961.
Jung, Carl G. *Man and His Symbols*. New York: Dell Publishing Co., Inc.,1964.
Jung, Carl G. *Memories, Dreams, Reflections*. New York: Vintage, 1965.
Kalakaua, David. *The Legends and Myths of Hawaii*. Tokyo: Charles E. Tuttle Co., l972.
Kenn, C. W. 1949. *Firewalking from the Inside*. Los Angeles: Franklin Thomas.
King, Serge V. 1976. *The Hidden Knowledge of Huna Science*. Santa Monica, California: Huna Enterprises
King, Serge V. 1979. *Kahuna Healing*. Malibu, California: Huna International

Long, Max Freedom. 1953. *The Secret Science at Work.* Los Angeles: Huna Research Publication.

Long, Max Freedom. 1954a. *Growing into Light.* Vista, California: Huna Research Publications.

Long, Max Freedom. 1954b. *The Secret Science Behind Miracles.* Los Angeles: DeVorss and Co.

Long, Max Freedom. 1958. *Self-Suggestion.* Marina del Rey, California: DeVorss and Co.

Long, Max Freedom. 1959. *Phychometric Analysis.* Marina del Rey, California: Devorss and Co.

Long, Max Freedom. 1965. *The Huna Code in Religions.* Santa Monica, California: Devorss.

Long, Max Freedom. 1975. *Introduction to Huna.* Vista, California: Huna Research Associates.

Long, Max Freedom 1978. *Short Talks on Huna.* Cape Girardeau, Missouri: Huna Press.

Long, Max Freedom. 1981a. *The Works of Max Freedom Long: HRA Bulletins.* Vol. 1. (Contains the HRA Bulletins written by Long from January, 1949-January, 1951.) Cape Girardeau, Missouri: Huna Research Associates.

Long, Max Freedom. 1981b. *The Works of Max Freedom Long: HRA Bulletins.* Vol. 2. (Contains the HRA Bulletins written by Long from January, 1951-January, 1953). Cape Girardeau, Missouri: Huna Research Associates.

Long, Max Freedom. 1981c. *The Works of Max Freedom Long: HRA Bulletins.* Vol. 3. (Contains the HRA Bulletins written by Long from January, 1953-July, 1959). Cape Girardeau, Missouri: Huna Research Associates.

Long, Max Freedom. 1981d. *The Works of Max Freedom Long: Huna Vistas.* Vol. 1. (Contains the Huna Vistas written by Long from September, 1959-September, 1962) . Cape Girardeau, Missouri: Huna Research Associates.

Long, Max Freedom. 1981e. *The Works of Max Freedom Long: Huna Vistas.* Vol. 2. (Contains the Huna Vistas written by Long from October, 1962-September, 1966). Cape Girardeau, Missouri: Huna Research Associates.

Long, Max Freedom. 1981f. *The Works of Max Freedom Long:Huna Vistas.* Vol. 3. (Contains the Huna Vistas written by Long from September, 1966-December, 1970). Cape Girardeau, Missouri: Huna Research Associates.

Maltz, Maxwell. *Psycho-Cybernetics.* Englewood Cliffs, New Jersey: Prentice-Hall, 1960.

Maltz, Maxwell. *Psycho-Cybernetics and Self-Fulfillment.* New

York: Grosset and Dunlap, 1970.

Mahesh Yogi, Maharishi. *Meditations of Maharishi Mahesh Yoga.* New York: Bantam Books, 1969.

Maslow, Abraham. *Religions, Values and Peak Experiences.* New York: Viking, 1970.

McBride, L. R. 1972. *The Kahuna, Versatile Mystics of Old Hawaii.* Hilo, Hawaii: The Petroglyph Press.

Melville, Leilani. 1969. *Children of the Rainbow.* Wheaton, Illinois: Quest Books. Quest Books.

Mishlove, Jeffrey. 1975. *The Roots of Consciousness: Psychic Liberation Through History, Science and Experience.* New York: Random House.

Montgomery, Ruth. 1976. *The World Before.* New York: Coward, McCann and Geoghegan, Inc.

Morrill, Sibley S., ed. 1968. *The Kahunas, the Black and White Magicians of Hawaii.* Boston: Branden Press.

Neihardt, John G. 1932. *Black Elk Speaks.* New York: Simon and Schuster.

The New Testament in Modern English. 1972. Edited by J. B. Phillips. New York: Mac Millan Publishing Co., Inc.

Ouspensky, P. D. *In Search of the Miraculous.* New York: Harcourt, Brace and World, 1949.

Patanjali. *How to Know God: The Yoga Aphorisms of Patanjali,* trans. and with a new commentary by Swami Prabhavananda and Christopher Isherwood. New York: Harper and Row, 1953.

Pearce, Joseph. *The Crack in the Cosmic Egg.* New York: Pocket Books, 1973.

Pearce, Joseph. *Magical Child.* New York: Bantam New Age Books, 1980.

Perls, Frederick S. *Gestalt Therapy Verbatim.* New York: Bantam, 1971.

Pukui, Mary Kawena, Samuel H. Elbert, and Esther T. Mookini, eds. 1975. *The Pocket Hawaiian Dictionary.* Honolulu: The University Press of Hawaii.

Pukui, Mary K., E. W. Haertig, and Catherine A. Lee. 1975. *Nana I Ke Kumu (Look to the Source).* Vols. 1 and 2. Honolulu: Hui Hanai

Reich Wilhelm. *History of the Discovery of Life Energy—The Einstein Affair.* Rangeley, Maine: Orgone Institute Press, 1953.

Rodman, Julius Scammon. 1979. *The Kahuna Sorcerers of Hawaii, Past and Present.* Hicksville, New York: Exposition

Press.

Self-Realization Fellowship. 1979. *Highway to the Infinite.* Los
    Angeles: Self-Realization Fellowship.

Stone, Margaret. 1979. *Supernatural Hawaii.* Honolulu: Aloha
    Graphics and Sales..

Sutphen, Dick. 1978. *Past Lives, Future Loves.* New York:
    Simon and Schuster.

Twitchell, Paul. 1975. *The Tiger's Fang.* Menlo Park, California:
    Illuminated Way Press.

Twitchell, Paul. 1980. *The ECK Satsang Discourses.* Menlo
    Park, California: Eckankar.

Wallis, Charles L., ed. 1965. *The Treasure Chest.* New York:
    Harper and Row.

Wharton, Nadine. 1970. Art of the Kahuna still lives: *Honolulu
    Star-Bulletin,* November 2, p. G-l.

Wingo, E. Otha. 1973. *Letters on Huna: A course in the
    Fundamentals of Huna Psychology.* Cape Girardeau,
    Missouri: Huna Research Associates.

Wingo, E. Otha, ed. *Huna Vistas Newsletter.* No. 35, HRA #262.
    Cape Girardeau, Missouri, September, 1980.

Wingo, E. Otha, ed. *Huna Vistas Newsletter.* No. 36, HRA #263.
    Cape Girardeau, Missouri, December, 1980.

Wingo, E. Otha, ed. *Huna Vistas Newsletter.* No. 1, HRA #265.
    Cape Girardeau, Missouri, June, 1981.

Yardley, Maili. *Hawaii Times and Tides.* Honolulu: Woolsey .
    Press, 1975.

Yogananda, Paramahansa. *Autobiography of a Yogi.* ,10th ed.
    Los Angeles: Self-Realization Fellowship, 1969.

Zambucka, Kristin. 1978. *Ano'Ano: The Seed.* Honolulu: Mana
    Publishing Co.

5

5

ORDER FORM

Send your request to:
Advanced Neuro Dynamics, Inc.
P.O. Box 3768 • Honolulu, Hawaii 96813

Customer toll free from the U.S. and Canada:
1-800-800-MIND (6463)
Direct: 1-808-521-0057 • Fax: 1-808-521-0051

NAME _____

ADDRESS _____

CITY/STATE _____ZIP _____

PHONE (   ) _____

____ Free catalog. ....FREE
____ Free information on Huna seminars with
Dr. Tad James and Dr. Laura Yardley ....FREE
____ **The Heart of Huna**
by Laura Yardley, PhD. Soft cover. (0.5 lb.) $9.95
____ **The Secret of Creating Your Future**
by Tad James, MS, PhD. Soft cover. (0.5 lb.) $9.95
____ **The Lost Secrets of Ancient Hawaiian Huna**
Intimate, introductory Huna presentation with Tad James.
Five audio cassettes and handouts. (1.5 lb.) $79.95

Sub total: _____

Hawaii residents add 4% tax: _____

Weight (lb.): ____ **Air Shipping** (from table below): _____

Total (U.S. funds): _____

Indicate method of payment:
__ Check   __ Money order   __ VISA   __ MasterCard   __ AMEX

Card No: _____

Expiration date: _____

Air Shipping

lbs	U.S.	Canada	A List	B List
0.5-1.5	$3.50	$5.00	$12.00	$16.00
2.0-2.5	$4.50	$7.00	$18.00	$22.50
3.0-4.5	$6.00	$8.00	$30.00	$35.00

A List: Western Europe, Hong Kong, Mexico, Venezuela
B List: All other countries. Subject to postal rate increases. Call if over 4.5 lbs.